Sports Economics, Management and Policy

Volume 17

Series Editor

Dennis Coates, Baltimore, MD, USA

The aim of this series is to provide academics, students, sports business executives, and policy makers with information and analysis on the cutting edge of sports economics, sport management, and public policy on sporting issues.

Volumes in this series can focus on individual sports, issues that cut across sports, issues unique to professional sports, or topics in amateur sports. Each volume will provide rigorous analysis with the purpose of advancing understanding of the sport and the sport business, improving decision making within the sport business and regarding policy toward sports, or both. Volumes may include any or all of the following: theoretical modelling and analysis, empirical investigations, or description and interpretation of institutions, policies, regulations, and law.

More information about this series at http://www.springer.com/series/8343

Jill S. Harris
Editor

The Economics of Aquatic Sports

Springer

Editor
Jill S. Harris
United States Air Force Academy
Colorado Springs, CO, USA

ISSN 2191-298X ISSN 2191-2998 (electronic)
Sports Economics, Management and Policy
ISBN 978-3-030-52339-8 ISBN 978-3-030-52340-4 (eBook)
https://doi.org/10.1007/978-3-030-52340-4

This Springer imprint is published by the registered company Springer Nature Switzerland AG
The registered company address is: Gewerbestrasse 11, 6330 Cham, Switzerland

This volume is dedicated to Coach Jeff Heidmous, Lt Col (Ret) United States Air Force. Coach Heidmous invested decades of time on and off the pool deck to shape collegiate water polo. He coached the United States Air Force Falcons for 25 seasons, leading the team to 3 conference championships, 5 NCAA appearances, and more than 300 wins. In the process, he mentored hundreds of athletes who eventually served their country as officers in the United States Air Force. I married one; I can vouch for the unique and lasting influence of Coach Heidmous.

Preface

This is a book about the particular economics of aquatic sports. But, it is really a book how economic forces are at work in all human behavior—inside and outside of the pool deck or natatorium. Human beings respond to incentives; the choices we make are generally always under conditions of scarce resources. Whether we are deciding which kind of bread to buy or whether or not to cheat by taking performance-enhancing drugs, we consider the potential benefits and costs. We do this with imperfect information and often in an environment where someone else has different or better information about the state of the world than we do. This makes human behavior (especially what we observe in sports) perpetually fascinating and worthy of study. This is also a book that illustrates how economists approach problems and questions about human behavior. Most, but not all, economists leverage the power of data to help us examine the questions we find interesting. The tools of data analysis continually evolve, but the basic framework is static. We ask a question or form a hypothesis, make a prediction, test the prediction, then repeat. This method of inquiry served us well for centuries. It is our hope that this volume inspires some group of athletes, scholars, administrators, coaches, and fans to continue studying the economics of sport—wherever it is found.

Colorado Springs, CO, USA — Jill S. Harris

Contents

Part I
Introduction to Aquatic Sport: Water Polo

Chapter 1
Do Aquatic Sports Make Much of a Splash?

Jill S. Harris

He's a water creature. You don't want him on land.
—Coach Bob Bowman.

Abstract The sports of water polo, swimming, and diving have not received as much attention as other high-profile sports like football. Yet, top athletes in these sports earn sizeable incomes and the organizing bodies of these sports exercise considerable power over economic outcomes. What follows is an introduction to some of the interesting economic questions involving aquatic sport—focusing on water polo and swim.

Before Michael Phelps dove into the Olympic scene, did anyone in the United States really care about swimming? Maybe. After the 1972 Olympics Mark Spitz (and his mustache) took home seven gold medals. Twelve years later, a 25-year-old Rowdy Gaines rallied during the 1984 Los Angeles games with three personal golds. However, it is arguably the story of Michael Phelps and his 28 Olympic medals (23 of them gold) that catapulted elite swimming back into the nation's spotlight. Adjusted for inflation, Phelps' $50 million plus in earnings from endorsements and sponsorships are more than double Spitz's career endorsement earnings. This is not surprising; Phelps' career spanned four Olympics (versus Spitz's two). He won his last medal as a 31-year-old athlete. Spitz earned his last Olympic gold as a 22-year-old athlete.[1] The impact of Phelps' career is not limited to dollars alone. Casual

[1] Spitz reportedly earned seven million dollars in endorsements in the two years following his retirement from swim (1972–1974). That translates into just over $41,000,000 in 2018 dollars. Michael Phelps' career endorsement earnings are estimated at $94,000,000. http://time.com/money/4459824/2016-rio-olympics-endorsement-deals/

J. S. Harris (✉)
United States Air Force Academy, Colorado Springs, CO, USA
e-mail: jill.harris@afacademy.af.edu

J. S. Harris (ed.), *The Economics of Aquatic Sports*, Sports Economics, Management and Policy 17, https://doi.org/10.1007/978-3-030-52340-4_1

investigation reveals a significant bump in age-group swimming participation after each of Phelps' Olympic appearances.

There are other spillover effects from Phelps' superstardom. It is not just that Phelps inspired more kids to jump into the lanes at their community pools. If you swim in the lane next to a faster swimmer, you swim faster. Phelps, quite literally, made everyone faster. In fact, in the most recent Olympics in Rio, the qualifying heats (with Phelps) were almost one full second faster than those without him. In a sport where Gold and Silver performances are separated by hundredths of a second, one full second is an eternity. Swimmers are faster now—there is no doubt about that. However, they are also earning more. This may be due to the peer effect of Phelps' higher income as well.

Although swimming, diving, and water polo are not as popular as basketball, football, and hockey, they can be lucrative for the top-performing athletes. Multimillion dollar endorsement deals are becoming the norm in swimming. In June of 2018, Katie Ledecky signed a $7 million marketing deal with TYR—the sponsor of the USA Swim Team. This contract lasts until 2024 and is being hailed as "one of the most lucrative" in the history of swimming.[2] Marketing tie-ins with watch companies, the nutrition industry, automobiles, and clothing lines are commonplace. In water polo, international club teams attracted star USA players like Tony Azevedo and Ryan Bailey (in the early 2000s). Tony's contract with the Italian club team, *Bissolati Cremona,* was $275,000 in 2004. This was more than double the previous record high contract for professional water polo players. Chris Ramsey, Chief Executive Officer of USA Water Polo, earns over $300,000 to manage that organization. This pales in comparison to the multimillion dollar endorsement deals in swimming, but is still a respectable salary in sport management. Table 1.1 summarizes some of the companies and athletes with multimillion dollar contracts.

Perhaps now that its elite athletes are making more money, aquatic sports are more intriguing. We can apply economic models of decision making to the sport to learn about the behavior of the governing organizations, labor markets, and

Table 1.1 Sample of elite swim and water polo earnings

Athlete	Company	Dollar amount
Michael Phelps	Louis Vuitton, Under Armour, Visa, Omega, Hilton, Proctor and Gamble, Subway, HP, Intel, Beats by Dre	$7–$12 million per year
Ryan Lochte	Gatorade, Gillette, Nissan, AT&T, Ralph Lauren, Speedo	$7–$8 million
Katie Ledecky Missy Franklin	TYR Speedo, Visa, Minute Maid, Go Pro, Wheaties, Topps, United Airlines, Penguin Random House	$7 million $3–5 million
Tony Azevedo	Bissolati Cremona	$275,000

[2] http://www.sportspromedia.com/news/katie-ledecky-big-first-pro-deal-tyr accessed 11 June 2018.

performance variables. After all, aquatic sports have many things in common with other industries (e.g., monopoly power in output markets and some price control over inputs). Recently, several members of USA swimming brought a class action suit against FINA—the governing body of international swim competition. [3] A new enterprise called the International Swim League was launched in 2019 by an energy mogul from Ukraine (Konstantin Grigorishin). FINA initially blocked swimmers from competing in this new league. FINA went so far as to threaten the athletes with denial of Olympic eligibility if they participated in the rival league contests. Aquatic sports organizations are sophisticated firms producing output under a variety of market structures. They are subject to the same antitrust rules as other professional and amateur sports leagues. Why should not we know more about how they work?

That is why we wrote this book. Whether you are interested in the hot-hand phenomenon, productivity analysis, referee bias, or the organization and behavior of sports leagues, you will find something to dive into these pages. While not exhaustive, this collection provides an introduction and overview of the economics of age group and collegiate and Olympic swimming, collegiate and Olympic water polo, the decision to use performance-enhancing drugs (PEDs), and the peculiar artifacts of the labor markets in each of these sports.

The book focuses on the world of water polo to begin (Part I). Chapter 2 introduces a simple model of wins produced in water polo. Those familiar with advanced analytics in basketball will immediately recognize the approach taken in this volume. The simple model provides one method for player and team evaluation. Eventually, this work can lead to labor studies involving player performance and pay.

Once player performance is summarized, it is often interesting to explore whether or not some players develop a hot hand during competition. Are water polo shooters "streaky" in the same way that basketball players are? Is the probability that a water polo goalie blocks the next shot increased if she blocks the prior shot? Questions about streakiness and momentum effects in general will be examined in Chapter 3.

The final two chapters in Part I investigate the specialization of labor in water polo and instances of referee bias. Why are international athletes (especially those from Croatia, Romania, and Hungary) recruited so heavily by college water polo teams? Similar to basketball, the best players are usually tall players, ceteris paribus. It turns out that people from these Eastern European countries are not only tall, but they have longer torsos than the rest of the population. This creates two of the three key characteristics in successful water polo players. As in other sports, referee behavior can be pivotal in the outcomes of water polo games. Chapter 4 reviews case evidence from championship tournaments, indicating that significant bias exists and can impact wins.

---

[3] *Shields,* et al. *v. FINA, Case No. 18-cv-07393 alleges that FINA is restricting completion by preventing its athletes from participating in the newly formed International Swim League sponsored events. The lawsuit seeks injunctive relief and monetary damages for all class members who signed initial contracts to swim in the rival league event. In December 2019, a San Francisco court denied FINA's request for dismissal of the suit.*

In Part II of the book, we dive into the economics of collegiate and professional swimming. Chapter 6 considers the substantial blocked entry effects of age group and collegiate swim programs. The market power exhibited by powerhouse swim schools inevitably leads to rent-seeking behavior. Chapter 7 estimates the impact of cartel power by calculating the deadweight welfare loss of the quota and price ceilings made possible by NCAA amateurism rules.

Due to the relative scarcity of swim scholarships and acceleration of qualifying times, PED use is common in swim and diving—just as it is in other highly competitive sports. Chapter 8 models this behavior as a strategic game and also considers the results of a Monte Carlo simulation of swimmer performance and medal earnings. How has technological change impacted swim performance? The introduction of the LZR Racer suit resulted in smashed world records and faster than ever swim finals. Chapter 9 investigates the impact before and after the suit was banned. This chapter also explores how rule changes around dolphin-kicks in the breaststroke changed performance and training regimens. The authors indicate that in both instances (technology and rule changes), the effects are different for male and female swimmers.

It is not surprising, perhaps, that monetary returns in aquatic competitions are different based on gender. This brings us full-circle to the earning potential for elite swimmers. We consider gender, age, and the effect of collegiate branding on financial returns in Chapter 10. Chapter 11 brings all the economics together for a final pass and review of the aquatic sport industry and points out several absorbing future paths for research.

References

Five Olympic Athletes with Insanely Big Endorsement Deals. (2016). Accessed July 17, 2018. http://time.com/money/4459824/2016-rio-olympics-endorsement-deals/

Katie Ledecky Secures Big First Pro Deal with TYR. (2018). Accessed June 11, 2018. http://www.sportspromedia.com/news/katie-ledecky-big-first-pro-deal-tyr

Shields v. Fed'n Internationale de Natation, Case No. 18-cv-07393-JSC (N.D. Cal. Dec. 16, 2019).

Chapter 2
Wins Produced in Water Polo

Jill S. Harris and David J. Berri

We swim well over 2 miles per match, we cannot touch the bottom of the pool, all while wrestling and fighting with another 6′ 5″, 250-lb. opponent.
—Shea Buckner, Team USA Water Polo Player

Abstract Measuring the productivity of labor in sport is often a difficult task. How do we separate the production of a quarterback from his offensive linemen, for example? In water polo, the task is made simple. Water polo is a complex invasion sport like basketball. Thus, we model the offensive and defensive efficiency of teams (as in Berri, Manag Decision Econ, 20(8): 411–427, 1999) in order to determine the impact of individual player effort on wins. From these results, we estimate the team wins produced and predict wins from eight seasons of collegiate water polo.

Ask anyone about water polo and you will likely hear some version of this reply: How do they get the horses in the water? The sport first emerged as a sort of water rugby in England and Scotland. The ball was made of Indian rubber; since the Balti word for ball was pronounced "pulu" by the British, the name water polo ultimately stuck to the sport.[1] Many fans are surprised to learn that water polo was among the original sports played in the Paris Olympic Games of 1900. Water polo is more widely played internationally than in the United States. Still, American Tony

[1] https://en.wikipedia.org/wiki/History_of_water_polo accessed 1 June 2018.

J. S. Harris (✉)
United States Air Force Academy, Colorado Springs, CO, USA

D. J. Berri
Southern Utah University, Cedar City, UT, USA

J. S. Harris (ed.), *The Economics of Aquatic Sports*, Sports Economics, Management and Policy 17, https://doi.org/10.1007/978-3-030-52340-4_2

Azevedo[2] is famous for leading three Olympic squads and playing competitive water polo in Brazil. The women's US Olympic team brought home gold medals in London in 2012 and Rio de Janeiro in 2016. Water Polo does not attract the crowds that professional soccer does. Water Polo does not have high-profile and dramatic salary negotiations like those between LeBron James and the Los Angeles Lakers. Yet, water polo is a professional sport. Men and women make a living at it. Athletes train hours a day and maintain rigorous nutritional and physical disciplines in order to perform at the highest levels. Economists study the productivity of labor in a variety of industries. It is time to study it in water polo.

In order to do this properly, we need to consider player performance statistics. Player statistics, according to Allen Barra,[3] are simply a summary of what players did when we were *not* watching them. They are records of the player's contributions to wins.[4] These contributions can be positive or negative. Once we gain an understanding of the player's contributions to wins, we can estimate the value of those contributions. Athlete performance in water polo is similar to that in basketball. A comparison of the two helps to set up our model of wins production.

Though the sport was once referred to as water rugby, it really is more closely related to basketball. In basketball, two teams of five players each try to acquire possession of the ball and advance it down the court in order to shoot the ball into a basket. Players execute offensive actions (i.e., shooting baskets, stealing the ball, passing the ball to another player, dribbling the ball) and defensive actions (i.e., blocking shots, drawing fouls). All of this is done within the limit of the shot clock set at 25 seconds. In water polo, two teams of seven players—six field players and one goalie—try to achieve the same objective: advancing the ball down the length of a pool to score a goal (or block a goal, in the case of the goalie). The pool dimensions vary between 20 × 10 meters and 30 × 20 meters. The goal is three meters wide and 90 centimeters high. Water polo has a 30-second shot clock limiting each offensive drive. The clock resets with a field blocked shot out-of-bounds or when the goalie blocks an attempt.

Basketball play can be interrupted by offensive and defensive fouls. The most innocuous of these simply causes play to be stopped and started again from the location of the foul. More serious violations result in turning the ball over to the opponent and chances for free throws. The same is true in water polo. Ordinary fouls (like impeding the free movement of a player not holding the ball) result in a momentary halt of play and player repositioning. Major fouls can result in an exclusion for the offending player for 20 seconds. Examples of these are holding, sinking,

[2]Azevedo played in five Olympic Games including the Silver Medal winning game in Beijing 2008. He has played on eight World Championship teams, earned five Pan American Game Gold Medals, and played in four FINA World Cup Tournaments and 12 World League Super Finals

[3]Allen Barra quoted in *Wages of Wins: Taking Measure of the Many Myths in Modern Sport* by Berri, Schmidt and Brook, p. 90.

[4]Berri and Schmidt (2010) made the following observation about why team's track statistics: "The primary purpose is to separate a player from his team. We know at the end of a contest who won. What we don't know is which players were responsible for a team's success (or failure)."

2017 Air Force Falcons Men's Water Polo Statistics

(9-14 Overall, 4-4 WWPA)

As of November 29, 2017 - All Games

##	Field Players	GP	Sh	G	A	PTS	ShPCT	EX	DEX	STL	FB	Sprint
15	Riley Thomas	21	122	46	27	73	.377	16	4	17	11	0-0
20	Justin Harrison	23	103	40	9	49	.388	11	17	7	2	0-0
18	Jack Empey	23	68	20	20	40	.294	12	5	8	5	0-0
6	Garrett Fisk	23	70	27	12	39	.386	15	41	18	6	0-1
12	Michael Miller	23	41	21	17	38	.512	7	9	17	5	37-20
9	Luke Andres	22	41	18	17	35	.439	14	11	18	5	0-0
23	Edward Smet	21	42	22	11	33	.524	9	1	13	0	0-0
14	Eric Kawecki	23	35	7	15	22	.200	6	1	14	5	0-0
7	Reagan Pittman	23	13	5	15	20	.385	6	1	11	1	0-0
25	Ryan Dorris	16	34	11	5	16	.324	16	1	5	10	0-0
8	George Millard	22	45	11	4	15	.244	6	1	10	4	0-1
16	Jason Hires	16	14	4	3	7	.286	9	1	6	2	0-1
21	Campbell Harris	17	7	2	3	5	.286	0	0	2	0	0-0
10	Neil Reynolds	22	16	2	2	4	.125	8	4	8	4	0-0
3	Jack Alexander	13	2	2	0	2	1.000	2	0	0	0	0-0
1A	James Burke	22	0	0	1	1	---	1	0	9	1	0-0
1	Nathan Kuypers	3	0	0	0	0	---	0	0	0	0	0-0
19	Owen Sedej	1	0	0	0	0	---	1	0	0	0	0-0
1B	Aiden Sandhu	5	0	0	0	0	---	0	0	2	0	0-0
4	Ben Gomez	11	0	0	0	0	---	1	0	0	0	0-0
11	Fabio Salvioni	1	0	0	0	0	---	0	0	0	0	0-0
	Totals		**653**	**238**	**161**	**399**	**.364**	**140**	**97**	**165**	**61**	**37-23**

##	Goaltenders	GP	GS	MIN	W	L	SA	SV	GA	SvPCT	GAA
1A	James Burke	21	18	633:00	9	11	439	198	241	.451	12.18
1	Nathan Kuypers	3	3	40:00	0	2	31	10	21	.323	16.80
1B	Aiden Sandhu	3	0	37:00	0	1	46	14	32	.304	27.68
	Totals			**710:00**	**9**	**14**	**516**	**222**	**294**	**.430**	**13.25**

Fig. 2.1 Water polo statistics as reported by the FOSH.net. GP is games played. Sh is shots taken, G is goals. A is assists. PTS are points. ShPCT is shot percentage. EX is exclusions (foul on the player). DEX is exclusions drawn (foul on opponent resulting in exclusion). STL is steals. FB is field block. Sprint is the race to the ball at a new period. For goaltenders: GP is games played, GS is games. MIN is minutes played. W is wins. L is losses. SA is saves attempted. SV is saves. GA is goals against. GAA is goals against average. SvPCT is save percentage

or pulling back a player who is not holding the ball. If these fouls occur outside the five-meter line, the player can take a free throw as a direct shot at the goal (defended only by the goalie). Figure 2.1 displays a sample stat sheet for Air Force Men's Water Polo for 2017.

Estimating the value of these different types of player labor is largely an exercise in determining the relative impact of each action on wins. The trick is to isolate each action, by holding the other actions constant, and then allow a small change in the isolated variable so that we can observe what happens to wins. For example, if a player steals one more ball from the opponent, what happens to wins, holding everything else constant?

In order to capture these effects, we build a model of wins by estimating the impact of offense and defense on wins.[5] First, at the most basic level, wins in water polo are a function of goals scored by the team and goals against by the opponents as Eq. 2.1 illustrates:

$$\boldsymbol{Wins = f\left(Goals\ Scored, Goals\ Against\right)} \tag{2.1}$$

Next, we break down how goals are scored. Goals are a result of players acquiring the ball and then putting the ball in play to score a goal. This means that goals are a function of turnovers, opponents' turnovers, and shooting efficiency for both teams. Thus, we estimate the impact on wins of the following:

$$\boldsymbol{Wins = f\begin{pmatrix} Attempts, Shot\ Efficiency, Opponent\ Shot\ Efficiency, \\ Turnovers, Opponent\ Turnovers \end{pmatrix}} \tag{2.2}$$

This approach is quite similar to that of Berri (1999, 2008).[6] The literature is brimming with examples of player performance models in basketball, baseball, and soccer.[7] There is less literature on wins produced in football. To date, no one we are aware of has formalized a model of wins produced in water polo. (In Chap. 4, however, Graham and Mayberry introduce a performance simulation model that estimates the impact of referee bias on wins).

The following steps are taken to develop a wins produced metric for field water polo players. First, we regress wins on measures of offensive and defensive efficiency—Eq. 2.2 above. This is done at the team level in order to develop weights for player actions in the pool. Next, we weight each player action by the estimated coefficients from the first regression equation. We adjust each weighted action by position. We do this because, as in basketball, a center in water polo plays closer to the goal and, other things the same, will draw more ejections (resulting in turnovers) and more scoring opportunities. Therefore, a center's production must be adjusted if we are to compare his productivity with that of a wing player (similar to shooting guard in basketball).

These steps give us a player's relative wins production. To convert this value to a total wins produced metric, we add this value to the value of wins an average player would produce. As in Berri (2008), if an average team wins 12 of 24 games in a season, and there are six field players, an average field player will produce two wins

---

[5] This approach directly echoes the approach taken by Gerrard (2007) to explore soccer and Berri (2008) to explore basketball.

[6] Berri (1999) describes an approach that was further refined in Berri, Schmidt, and Brook (2006) and Berri (2008). The approach taken by Berri echoes the approach taken by Gerrard (2007). The work of Gerrard (2007) details how one models what Gerrard refers to as a "complex invasion sport" (i.e. soccer, basketball, hockey, American football, and water polo). See also, Berri (1999). Berri (2008).

[7] See Berri and Simmons (2011), Berri et al. (2007), Sampaio and Janeira (2003), Todd Jewell and Molina (2004).

(i.e., 12 games divided by six players). This production must be adjusted for the amount of time the player spends in the pool. Suppose out of the 32 minutes of collegiate game play an average player spends 16 minutes in the game. Then, the average player's contribution to wins is one game. Last, we adapt the performance metric for team defensive statistics. This is done in the standard way in the literature by allocating the team defensive adjustment for the time each player is in the pool.

This water polo wins produced model uses data from Division I College water polo. Specifically, it uses data from the Western Water Polo Association (WWPA) conference for the years 2010–2017. Seven teams played 12–24 games each season[8]. After eliminating players with missing statistics, and teams with missing observations for some years, this study includes 980 player year observations, and 42 team year observations.

Summary statistics for key variables in the data set are captured in Table 2.1.

Teams in the WWPA in this time period are evenly matched. On average, they have similar amounts of turnovers and attempts and the shot efficiency measures are also consistent across the league. As we would expect, the average win percent is 50%, with the lowest performing teams in the sample winning just 25% of their games (Fresno Pacific and Loyola Marymount) and the best performing team (UC Davis) winning 71% of its games.

Results from regressions on Eqs. 2.1 and 2.2 are summarized in Table 2.2.

These estimates were obtained without considering goalie defensive efforts. This basic model explains about 55% of the variation in win percentage in the sample. Additional models are needed to incorporate the impact of goalie play on wins. Even so, the results reported here align with similar models in basketball. Shooting efficiency has the most impact on wins. If a team can increase its efficiency by one percentage point, then its winning percentage will go up by almost two percentage points. The other statistics have the predicted signs and relative magnitudes we expect from a complex invasion sport model of wins produced.

Table 2.1 Summary statistics for n = 980 player year observations

Variable	Mean	Std. dev.	Min	Max
Attempts	715	175	385	1184
Opponent attempts	704	72	385	849
Shot efficiency	0.406	0.087	0.274	0.603
Opponent shot efficiency	0.400	0.070	0.259	0.613
Turnovers	244	75	104	390
Opponent turnovers	237	27	185	289
Win percent	0.499	0.119	0.250	0.708

[8] Teams include Air Force, California Baptist University, Fresno Pacific University, Loyola Marymount University, Santa Clara University, UC Davis, and UC San Diego.

Table 2.2 The value of water polo statistics in terms of win percentage

Water polo statistic	If each variable increased by 1	If each variable increased by 100
Goals	0.001	0.10
Attempts	0.001	0.10
Opponent attempts	−0.000363	−0.04
Turnovers	−0.000480	−0.05
Opponent turnovers	0.001042	0.10
Shot efficiency[a]	0.018	1.80

[a]Shot efficiency is a ratio of goals/attempts. It is expressed in terms of percentage. To evaluate the marginal impact of a one unit increase in efficiency we examine whether goals increase per attempt, or attempts decreas per goals scored. Therefore, a one percent increase in shot efficiency increases win percentage by 1.8 percentage points, while a 100 percent increase in shot efficiency increases win percentage by 180 percentage points

Using these estimated coefficients, a model of team wins can be produced as described above. Table 2.3 summarizes the predictions for the 2017 men's WWPA water polo season[9]:

For the 2017 season, the model of wins produced predicts outcomes fairly well. If we consider the absolute value of the difference between the predicted and actual wins for the season, overall the average absolute error is 1.31 games. Given a season of roughly 24 games, the error is 5% of the total. (The model predicts wins from prior seasons with similar average absolute errors). We speculate the error has something to do with goalie performance. Additional models are needed to capture the impact of these actions on wins.

There are several important future directions for this wins produced research. First, the model can be applied to the rest of the Division I men's and women's water polo teams. We know that wins impact recruiting efforts, coaching salaries, coach retention, and donor behavior. All of this could be investigated with the help of our wins produced model. Second, the model can be extended with goalie performance analytics. Given the reasonable results from field player analysis in the WWPA conference, we expect that with more data across more conferences and the addition of the goalie production, the model will be even more robust. Third, the model can be used to study Olympic level performance. Many studies examine the relative performance of players in order to rank them (i.e., draft picks, All-Star team selection, most valuable player status, etc.).[10] This study can contribute to Olympic

[9]We only included games played in tournaments where the conference teams also participated. For example, Cal Baptist hosts a Lancer Joust tournament; these games (and wins) are not counted here, because WWPA schools did not participate.

[10]See Berri et al. (2011). Also see, Harris and Berri (2015).

Table 2.3 Sample predictions from wins produced model in the WWPA 2017 season

Team	Sum of player wins produced	Actual team wins	Difference in absolute terms
Air Force	10.19	10	0.19
California Baptist	12.33	11	1.33
Fresno Pacific	5.22	6	0.78
Loyola Marymount	7.23	6	1.23
Santa Clara	11.04	8	3.04
UC Davis	15.34	17	1.66
UC San Diego	11.97	11	0.97

Average absolute error: 1.31

team selection decisions and team management decisions in terms of minutes played. Future studies might include an examination into racial or country of origin bias on the part of Olympic coaches, for example. Finally, we might be able to learn something about momentum effects and the so-called hot hand by studying water polo through a wins produced lens. The next chapter provides an introduction to this contentious phenomenon in the sport of water polo.

References

Berri, D. J. (1999). Who is 'most valuable'? Measuring the player's production of wins in the National Basketball Association. *Managerial and Decision Economics, 20*(8), 411–427.

Berri, D. J. (2008). A simple measure of worker productivity in the national basketball association. In B. Humphreys & D. Howard (Eds.), *The business of sport* (Vol. 3, pp. 1–40). Westport: Praeger.

Berri, D. J., & Schmidt, M. B. (2010). *Stumbling on wins: Two economists explore the pitfalls on the road to victory in professional sports*. Princeton: Financial Times Press.

Berri, D. J., & Simmons, R. (2011). Catching a draft: On the process of selecting quarterbacks in the National Football League amateur draft. *Journal of Productivity Analysis, 35*(1), 37–49.

Berri, D. J., Schmidt, M. B., & Brook, S. L. (2006). *The wages of wins: Taking measure of the many myths in modern sport*. Stanford University Press. Released in paperback in September, 2007.

Berri, D. J., Brook, S. L., & Schmidt, M. B. (2007). Does one simply need to score to score? *International Journal of Sport Finance, 2*(4), 190.

Berri, D. J., Brook, S. L., & Fenn, A. J. (2011). From college to the pros: Predicting the NBA amateur player draft. *Journal of Productivity Analysis, 35*(1), 25–35.

Gerrard, B. J. (2007). Is the *Moneyball* approach transferable to complex invasion team sports? *International Journal of Sport Finance, 2*(4), 214–230.

Harris, J., & Berri, D. J. (2015). Predicting the WNBA draft: What matters most from college performance? *International Journal of Sport Finance, 10*(4), 299.

Sampaio, J., & Janeira, M. (2003). Statistical analyses of basketball team performance: understanding teams' wins and losses according to a different index of ball possessions. *International Journal of Performance Analysis in Sport, 3*(1), 40–49.

Todd Jewell, R., & Molina, D. J. (2004). Productive efficiency and salary distribution: The case of US Major League Baseball. *Scottish Journal of Political Economy, 51*(1), 127–142.

Chapter 3
Hot Hands in Cold Water

Jill S. Harris and James Graham

> *After the game, a stunned (Draymond) Green was asked whether someone could possibly do that in the "NBA 2K" video game. His response? "Nah, you don't get that hot in 2K."*
> —Draymond Green talking about Klay Thompson's hot hand in the January 23, 2015 game against the Sacramento Kings.

Abstract Cross-sectional data from a NCAA Division 1 Men's and Women's water polo program is used to investigate the "myth" of the hot hand. Following the pioneering work of Gilovich et al. (Cognitive Psychol 17: 295–314, 1985), analysis of conditional probabilities, serial correlation, and runs reveals partial evidence in support of the hot hand on both individual and aggregate levels. The results are counter to Gilovich et al. and potentially important in light of Wardrop's (Am Stat 49: 24–28, 1999) critiques and recent work by Arkes (J Q Anal Sports 6(1), 2010) and Stone (Am Stat 66(1):61–66, 2012), indicating these approaches lack power and are subject to measurement error. A probit model of shots is estimated using player fixed effects. The results suggest player position, and experience together with the sequence of the shot in the series all influence the likelihood of successful shots.

Introduction

Water polo may seem an unlikely sport for hot-hand research. Basketball, baseball, golf, bowling, soccer, volleyball, and even darts serve this purpose in the recent literature (Gilovich et al. 1985; Arkes 2013; Stone 2012; Albright 1993; Livingston

J. S. Harris (✉)
United States Air Force Academy, Colorado Springs, CO, USA
e-mail: jill.harris@afacademy.af.edu

J. Graham
University of the Pacific, Stockton, CA, USA

J. S. Harris (ed.), *The Economics of Aquatic Sports*, Sports Economics, Management and Policy 17, https://doi.org/10.1007/978-3-030-52340-4_3

2012; Yaari and Eisenmann 2011; Raab et al. 2011; Otting and Deutscher 2018). Yet, water polo has some of the same features (multiple players and attempted shots) and offers one additional benefit (like soccer does): the use of goalies. Although water polo may be a lower scoring event overall compared to basketball, goalies are constantly defending. Their blocked shots (saves) and missed blocks (goals) can be included in analysis of hits and misses to investigate the hot hand as well. Due to the smaller dimensions of the pool, water polo goalies face more attempted shots than soccer goalies. It is very likely water polo players, coaches, and fans suffer from cognitive error and misunderstanding of randomness while they play, supervise, and enjoy the game. Or, as we hint at here, they could be viewing players that are truly "hot."

Psychologists, economists, and other decision theory scholars have been debating the hot-hand question for decades (see Bar-Eli et al. 2006, for a review). Attention in the popular press via such titles as *Naked Economics*, *Thinking Fast and Slow*, and *Nudge* has made the topic accessible to a wider audience (this is noted in Arkes 2013). Despite the mostly negative reporting on hot-hand effect in these titles, one of the unintended consequences of their popularity is an increase in the perceived value of studying human nature within the world of sport. Nearly all of the referenced literature discusses the implications of the hot hand in sport for other human activities (i.e., investment behavior, teamwork, strategic planning).

Considerable disagreement remains though about the appropriate tests for measuring the hot hand (Dorsey-Palmateer and Smith 2004; Miyoshi 2000; Wardrop 1999) and the power and precision of the originating methods by Gilovich et al. (Arkes 2013, Stone 2012). Still, the consensus is there is not compelling evidence of the hot (or cold) hand nor of momentum effects (Camerer 1989; Brown and Sauer 1993; Vergin 2000; Hendricks et al. 1993; Elton et al. 1996; Metrick 1999). Recent threads of the literature have leveraged the power of larger databases and simulations across all players versus single players to find a small but statistically significant hot-hand effect in basketball free throws (Arkes 2013). Using a hypergeometric distribution of individual and aggregated results, Yaari and Eisenmann (2011) confirm and extend the results in Arkes (2010). In Albright (1993), a model including player situational variables and sequencing of at-bats in baseball indicates "streaky behavior" like the hot hand on the individual level, but fails to establish such in the aggregate. Our study fits into this niche in the literature; it considers both individual players' and group performance using both the earlier approaches (conditional probability, correlation, and runs tests) and a probit model with player-specific variables. Unlike the results of the study of Albright (1993) and Gilovich et al. (1985), these results suggest that a hot-hand effect is present at the individual *and* aggregate levels and could provide some insight into the likelihood of successful shots. It is an important case study for two reasons. First, the sample size is much smaller than those utilized in prior work. This is relevant because both Arkes (2013) and Stone (2012) find sample size to be a limiting factor in hot-hand studies. (Hence, the focus on simulations). If this case study tests for and finds a hot hand in players or teams with roughly four percent of the sample size other work used, then a re-examination of the hot hand in other sports is warranted. Second, if the hot-hand effect is present and statistically significant in water polo data, then the probability model could help identify what factors contribute to it. These insights can also help us understand more about the hot hand in complex invasion sports.

Method

Unlike previous studies using borrowed data sets, this paper examines author-generated data from a tournament of men's and women's water polo at a top 20 Division 1 program. Generally, goals per game, saves per game (for goalies), fouls, ejections, exclusions drawn (fouls on opponents), and scores are collected. Testing the null hypothesis of "no hot hand" requires sequence data if the shots are sampled from live games. Game films were reviewed and data on shot attempts, goals ("hits" in the literature), the sequence of shots in the game, fouls, exclusions, and several other variables were recorded per player.

Water polo can be a low scoring event relatively speaking. For example, in the current season of data, there are almost as many games in single digits (9–6 win) as double (12–8 win). With 6 players in the field, the distribution of shot attempts and hits can be fairly wide across the team. As with other sports, substitutions are made periodically, which can reduce the number of attempts and goals for the starters; thus, not every game in the season is optimal for the purposes of investigating streaks in shooting. Still, goalies provide compensating activity; they block the opponents' attempted shots. So, even for lower scoring games, there is a reasonable number of observations for analysis. The current sample includes observations drawn from 10 games across 16 players ($N = 428$). These were narrowed to observations from 10 games across 12 players for the probability, correlations, and runs tests. Players with fewer than 10 combined attempted shots were dropped. The full sample was included in the probit model.

Once the game stats were recorded, the data was coded into one large cross-sectional set. Although the data can be described as a time series (each game serving as the time period), for purposes of this study, it seemed conservative to interpret the data as cross-sectional (one season as the time period). Details are explained below. After the data was assembled, conditional probabilities for the 12 players' performance (Hit/Miss, Hit/Hit, Miss/Hit, Miss/Miss) were calculated. In addition, a correlation coefficient was estimated and a runs test was performed on each player's data individually and in the aggregate following Gilovich, et al. The runs test statistic is:

$$Z = \left(R - \mu_R\right) / \sigma_R$$

where R is the number of runs in a sequence, μ_R is the mean, and σ_R is the standard deviation. The decision rule is to reject the null hypothesis of independence (randomness) if $Z \geq 1.645$. If a player is "hot," then in a particular series of shots, successes should be clustered. For example, if the player events look like this:

11001011110110000011

the number of runs for this series is nine. Therefore, if the number of runs in the sample is smaller than the expected runs under the null hypothesis of independence or randomness, the null is rejected.

Finally, a probit model of the general form $p = \Phi(\beta 1 + \beta 2X)$ was used (as in Hill, Griffiths, Lim *Principles of Econometrics* 2008), where p is the probability the dependent variable (successful shot) takes the value 1, Φ is the probit function, $\beta 1$ and $\beta 2$ are parameters to be estimated, and X is a set of variables impacting the likelihood of successful shots detailed in the next section.

Data

The data set includes 428 observations on 16 variables. Summary statistics on key variables are summarized in Table 3.1:

Figures 3.1 and 3.2 provide context for the sample data. The attempted shots from our sample are in blue. The goals for the sample are in red and the goals for the season are in green. Player performance for the season is depicted in light green. Figure 3.1 compares the shot attempts and goals for the field players (numbered 1–10 on the horizontal axis), while Fig. 3.2 shows the goalie performance measures.

Player 1 took 25 shots and scored 10, which translates into 40% "efficiency" for the sample period. This player had a 32% efficiency for the entire season. Every player's efficiency for the sample period was within 10% of their season efficiency. The one exception was player 7; this player's efficiency was 25% during the sample and improved to 48% for the season. This difference is likely explained by position (as a center, the player takes more shots over the course of a season and is more likely to make more shots over the season). Overall, the sample-to-season comparisons provide some assurance that the shot taking in the sample is reasonably indicative of the shot-taking over the season.

Table 3.1 Summary statistics from the tournament data

Variable	Mean	St. Dev.	Min–max
Shotb	0.521	0.500	0–1
Female	0.544	0.498	0–1
Position	4.890	2.305	1–7
Exp	1.337	0.701	0–2.25
Period 2	0.299	0.458	0–1
Period 3	0.259	0.438	0–1
Period 4	0.161	0.368	0–1

Summary statistics for $n = 428$ observations SHOTb = dummy variable equal to 1 for blocked shot or goal scored, 0 otherwise. FEMALE = dummy variable equal to 1 if female player, 0 otherwise. POSITION = number assigned to player zone in pool ranges from 1 to 7. EXP = an interactive term capturing years of experience with goals per game. PERIOD 2,3,4 = 1 for each period, 0 otherwise

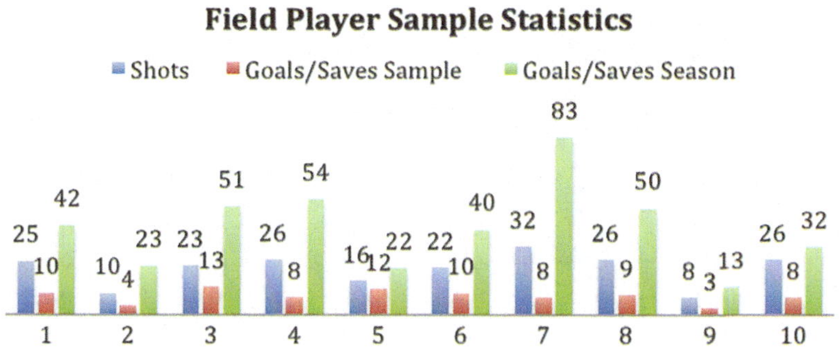

Fig. 3.1 Shows sample shot attempts in blue with goals from the sample (red) and goals for the entire season (green)

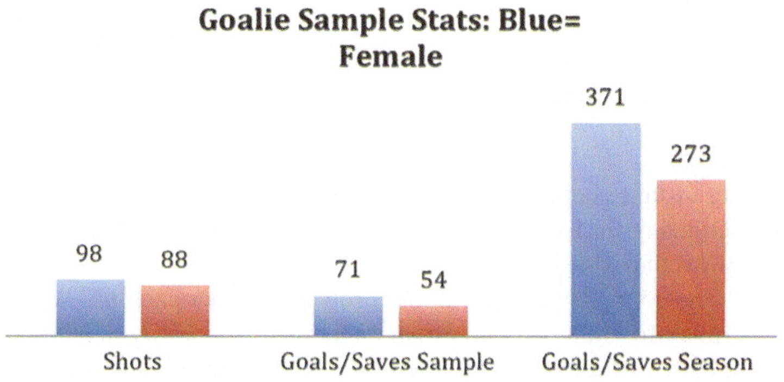

Fig. 3.2 Shows sample shots attempted, saves made in the sample, and saves made for the season.

The goalie sample reflects the overall season performances. It is not uncommon for female goalies to block more shots than male counterparts. Female athletes have less speed on the ball than male players. For any given game, both male and female goalies experience a much higher number of events than field players. In addition, the goalie's performance may be the most potentially impacted by game situations like penalty shots, exclusions (6 on 5 play), fouls, and turnovers. These features make a number of other interesting research questions plausible. A couple of these will be addressed in the discussion section.

Tests

Gilovich, et al. found only one instance of positive serial correlation and attributed it to random chance; there are two instances of positive correlation in the sample as shown in Table 3.2. However, only one is significant (Player 7). An asterisk on the reported p-value indicates statistical significance at the 10%, 5% or 1% level.

Table 3.2 Conditional probabilities and correlation coefficients

Player	H/M	H/H	M/H	M/M	rho	p-value
1	0.24	0.73	0.62	0.26	−0.22	0.812
2	0.5	0.7	0.33	0.6	0.27	0.630
3	0.41	0.52	0.61	0.29	−0.49	0.000*
4	0.75	0.25	0.33	0.66	−0.09	0.737
5	0.53	0.61	0.46	0.2	−0.21	0.170
6	0.62	0.38	0.33	0.72	0.13	0.499
7	0.15	0.75	0.41	0.6	0.418	0.039*
8	0.71	0.5	0.58	0.16	−0.28	0.166
9	0.75	0.25	0.25	0.56	−0.01	0.990
10	0.77	0.22	0.36	0.71	−0.51	0.060*
11	0.66	0.33	0.4	0.4	−0.17	0.501
12	0.86	0.25	0.33	0.5	−0.49	0.058*
Sample					0.3068	0.001

Three other instances of correlation are significant but suggest the opposite of the hot hand: a tendency for hits to follow misses. At best, this first test is inconclusive and may confirm the same result as Gilovich, et al.

Table 3.2 also contains the conditional probabilities for each player of four scenarios: the probability of a hit conditional on a miss, probability of a hit conditional on a hit, probability of a miss conditional on a hit, and probability of a miss conditional on miss. The probabilities show a mixed bag of results. Players 2 and 7 are the only clear examples of higher conditional probabilities of hits following hits and misses following misses. Players 1, 3, 5 have conditional probabilities of hits following hits that are higher than following misses. Taken together, 5 of the 12 in the sample exhibit—at least partially—what could be labeled a hot-hand effect according to this test.

Lastly, Table 3.3 reports the hits, misses, runs, expected number of runs, and Z stat for each player. An asterisk on the reported p-values indicates statistical significance at the 10%, 5% or 1% level.

Five players possess fewer than the expected number of runs under the hypothesis of independence and one additional player has an insignificant difference in runs in the opposite direction. Overall, the number of runs for the entire sample is less than expected (157 runs is smaller than the 215 expected under independence) with a Z stat of -1.742 and p-value 0.081. Clearly, this is counter to Gilovich, et al. and perhaps surprising given the smaller sample size, but not altogether counterintuitive given the mixed results from the prior tests.

Table 3.3 Hit, misses, and actual and expected runs

Player	Hits	Misses	# Runs	Expected runs	Z	*p*-value
1	71	27	41	50	−1.92	0.055*
2	10	15	11	13.5	−1.02	0.307
3	54	34	14	13	0.417	0.64
4	4	6	6	6	0	1
5	13	10	14	12.5	0.639	0.522
6	8	18	9	13	−1.67	0.095*
7	12	5	5	9	−2.07	0.038*
8	10	12	15	12.5	1.309	0.19
9	8	24	12	16.5	−1.64	0.1*
10	9	17	14	14	0	1
11	3	5	3	4	−2.85	0.004*
12	8	18	13	14	−0.4	0.689
Sample	210	191	157	215	−1.742	0.0814*

Probit Results

We think the results of the runs test point to the possibility of a hot hand in water polo for the tournament we studied. Which variables in our data set are most likely to influence the probability of making a shot (or blocking a shot if a goalie)? Table 3.4 shows the results of a probit model of shot success.

In this sample, FEMALE is not significant. Gender does not appear to influence the probability of shot success. The impact of SEQUENCE is small, but consistently of value in the model for predicting the probability of successful shots. To be clear, as modeled, SEQUENCE and other variables are not predicting the likelihood of the hot hand—a streak itself—but rather the likelihood of a successful shot, which may contribute to a streak or the hot hand. Here, it seems that as players progress through the game, they are more likely to make successful shots after other shots are made versus before a large number of shots. This makes intuitive sense; players are warming up, sizing up the defense, learning as they play about the game dynamics. Note that SEQUENCE may or may not be correlated with periods of play. For example, some games may see a hyperactive second period with 20 shots, whereas the fourth period may only see five.

P5meter is not significant in this sample. This variable records penalty shots. A five-meter penalty is awarded when a major foul occurs within five meters of the goal or when a clear opportunity to score is denied. This shot is taken by the opposing team on the five-meter line in front of the goal. Two defensive players are lined up with the opposing player. If the goalies blocks the ball, the ball is live and play continues. Blocking a five-meter shot can be psychologically powerful for goalies and for a team that is behind. For future studies, a lagged P5meter variable may be a better predictor for field player as well as goalie success, since a successful block

Table 3.4 Results from probit model

SHOTB is dependent variable				
Variable	Coefficient	Std. Error	T-ratio	*P*-value
Sequence	*0.019*	*0.007*	*2.504*	*0.012***
p 5 meter	*0.806*	*0.604*	*1.334*	*0.182*
Position	*0.081*	*0.035*	*2.335*	*0.020***
Period 3	*−0.32*	*0.201*	*−1.568*	*0.117*
Period 4	*−0.75*	*0.277*	*−2.713*	*0.001****
Exp	*0.35*	*0.115*	*3.063*	*0.002***
	N = 428			

Probit model for $n = 428$ observations SHOTb = dummy variable equal to 1 for blocked shot or goal scored, 0 otherwise. SEQUENCE = a positive number indicating when the shot occurred during the game. P 5 METER = dummy variable equal to 1 if the shot was for a five-meter penalty. POSITION = number assigned to player zone in pool ranges from 1 to 7. EXP = an interactive term capturing years of experience with goals per game. PERIOD 2,3,4 = 1 for each period, 0 otherwise. *** = 1% level of significance. ** = 5% level of significance.

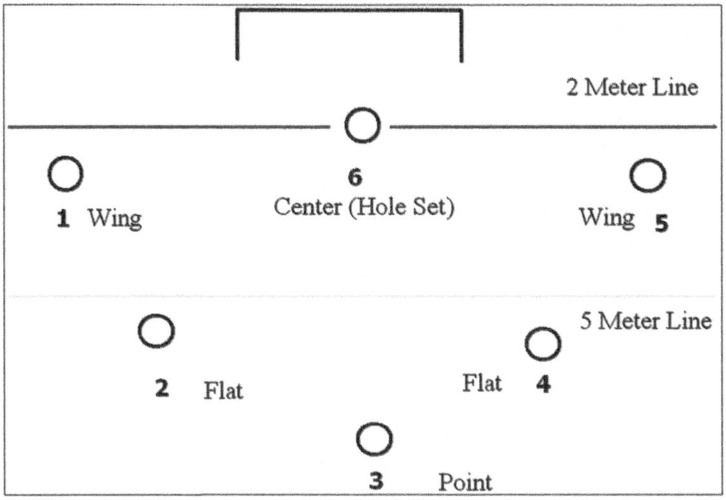

Fig. 3.3 Typical Setup for water polo

on a 5 meter shot usually "fires" up the goalie and the team (i.e., if all of the above are not suffering from cognitive illusion!)

POSITION positively impacts the likelihood of success. Consider Fig. 3.3 on a typical team setup

For right-handed shooters, it is much easier to shoot a successful goal from positions 2–5 with the optimal zone occurring between 3 and 4. For lefties, the conditions are different. Position 6 is closest to the goal but defended the most vigorously. Position 7 in our sample is the goalie and since we have established, they experience much more activity; we would expect Position 7 to have the highest probability for successful shots (blocked goals).

Period 4 and Period 3 negatively impact the likelihood of success in the sample. While this result seems to conflict with the discussion on SEQUENCE above, the two results need not be mutually exclusive. SEQUENCE may or may not be related to the strict time periods marked by this dummy variable. Therefore, it could be that players are tired by this time and less effective (most starters play a majority of the game). However, it could also be true that more substitutions are made in later periods—especially if there is a sizeable lead. This was the case for a couple games in our sample. Thus, with the sample players playing fewer minutes in the later periods, the probabilities of success could be negatively affected.

Finally, EXP positively influences the likelihood of success. This means that as the experience of the player on the team increases (as captured by their age and historical performance), the probability of making a successful shot increases.

Conclusion

Tests for the hot-hand effect have been limited in the past by small sample sizes and power. Current research exploiting larger data sets with more powerful tests has found instances of the hot hand or has established that prior methods may have been subject to measurement error. In light of these findings, our results are meaningful for two reasons. First, by comparison to prior research, the current sample is relatively small ($N = 428$ versus $N = 727$ in Gilovich, et al). Both the probabilities and runs test statistic indicate plausible hot-hand effects. Indeed, the run test results suggest the potential presence of the hot hand for five out of twelve players in the sample. The second meaningful result is that factors like experience, positioning, and sequencing could impact the probability of shot success. This result has obvious applications within the sport of water polo for coaching and strategy. Coaches obviously want to have the right players in the pool at the right time and in the right place. Feedback about experience, position, and sequence can provide coaches with better information when putting together their rosters or making substitutions during a game.

Applying this same type of analysis to, say, brokers on a stock exchange floor or a group of acquisition contractors in the government might result in better outcomes. Team leaders want to have the right team members on the right assignment at the right time. Studying the experience, positioning within a team, and sequencing of team moves might identify brokers and contractors who are "hot" versus those who are not.

Two immediate directions for future research emerge. First, these results should be merged with a wins produced model (like that introduced in Chapter Two) in order to create a more robust total model of performance in water polo. A second line of inquiry for future research focuses on center and goalie performance. Goalies usually play the entire game; they block attempted goals and allow shots that become goals. From the fan perspective, these two features of goalie play can make it appear that the goalie is "hot" or "cold." Similarly, centers—by virtue of being physically closest to the goal and anchoring the offense—handle the ball more than other field players. Future research should focus on the players with their hands on the ball most often to confirm whether or not there are hot hands in cold water.

References

Albright, S. C. (1993). A statistical analysis of hitting streaks in baseball. *Journal of the American Statistical Association, 88*, 1175–1183.

Arkes, J. (2010). Revisiting the hot hand theory with free throw data in a multivariate framework. *Journal of Quantitative Analysis in Sports, 6*(1).

Arkes, J. (2013). Misses in "Hot Hand" Research. *Journal of Sports Economics 14*(4):401–410.

Bar-Eli, M., Avugos, S., & Raab, M. (2006). Twenty years of "hot hand" research: Review and critique. *Psychology of Sport and Exercise, 7*(6), 525–553.

Brown, W. O., & Sauer, R. D. (1993). Does the basketball market believe in the hot hand - comment. *American Economic Review, 83*, 1377–1386.

Camerer, C. F. (1989). Does the basketball market believe in the hot hand. *American Economic Review, 79*, 1257–1261.

Dorsey-Palmateer, R., & Smith, G. (2004). Bowlers' hot hands. *The American Statistician, 58*, 38–45.

Elton, E. J., Gruber, M. J., & Blake, C. R. (1996). The persistence of risk-adjusted mutual fund performance. *Journal of Business, 69*, 133–157.

Gilovich, T., Vallone, R., & Tversky, A. (1985). The hot hand in basketball: On the misperception of random sequences. *Cognitive Psychology, 17*, 295–314.

Hendricks, D., Patel, J., & Zeckhauser, R. (1993). Hot hands in mutual funds: Short-run persistence of relative performance, 1974–1988. *Journal of Finance, 48*(1), 93–130.

Hill, C., Griffiths, B., & Lim, G. (2008). *Principles of econometrics*. Hoboken, NJ, John Wiley & Sons, Inc.

Kahneman, D. (2011). *Thinking fast and slow*. New York, NY, Farar Strauss Giroux.

Livingston, J. A. (2012). The hot hand and the cold hand in professional golf. *Journal of Economic Behavior & Organization, 81*(1), 172–184.

Metrick, A. (1999). Performance evaluation with transaction data: The stock selection of investment newletters. *Journal of Finance, 54*, 1743–1775.

Miyoshi, H. (2000). Is the "hot hands" phenomenon a misperception of random events? *Japanese Psychological Research, 42*, 128–133.

Nickerson, R. S. (2002). The production and perception of randomness. *Psychological Review, 109*, 330–357.

Otting, L., & Deutscher, L.-B. (2018). The hot hand in professional darts. *Journal of the Rogyal Statistical Society: Series A (Statistics in Society), 1803*.

Raab, M., Gula, B., & Gigerenzer, G. (2011). The hot hand exists in volleyball and is used for allocation decisions. *Journal of Experimental Psychology: Applied*. [PubMed].

Stone, D. F. (2012). Measurement error and the hot hand. *The American Statistician, 66*(1), 61–66.

Vergin, R. C. (2000). Winning streaks in sports and the misperception of momentum. *Journal of Sport Behavior, 23*(2), 181–197.

Wardrop, R. L. (1999). *Statistical tests for the hot-hand in basketball in a controlled setting*. http://www.stat.wisc.edu/_wardrop/papers/tr1007.pdf

Yaari, G., & Eisenmann, S. (2011). The hot (invisible?) hand: Can time sequence patterns of sucess/failure in sports be modeled as repeated random independent trials? *PLoS One, 6*(10), e24532.

Chapter 4
The Cost of Losing Team Bias in Water Polo

James Graham and John Mayberry

I do not look back at what might have been. If I did that, playing golf would drive me crazy.

—Tiger Woods

Abstract Parallel game simulations are utilized to determine whether or not bias in foul calling can impact the outcomes of games. The authors find that referees, not team performance, may be the source of losing team bias.

Official Bias

Official bias is now a well-established phenomenon in almost all major sports. Forty years of quantitative research into this area has supported common stereotypes that referees tend to favor the home team (Nevill and Holder 1999), are adverse to sequential calls against the same team (Anderson and Pierce 2009; Noecker and Roback 2012), and, in some situations, are supportive of the underdog (Brymer et al. 2015). In addition, referees in many sports seem to have an innate tendency to favor the losing team. For example, in NCAA basketball, it has been shown that foul calls are more likely to go against the losing team (Anderson and Pierce 2009) and in soccer, it has been shown that losing teams are more likely to receive penalty kicks (Plessner and Betsch 2001). In baseball, a similar effect is also present in strike calling patterns: strike zones tend to increase when the batter is up in the count and decrease when the batter is down (Moskowitz and Wertheim 2012; Green and Daniels 2014).

Elite water polo provides a particularly interesting forum for investigating officiating for two reasons. First, as Fig. 4.1 demonstrates, more than half of all goals in

J. Graham · J. Mayberry (✉)
University of the Pacific, Stockton, CA, USA
e-mail: jmayberry@pacific.edu

J. S. Harris (ed.), *The Economics of Aquatic Sports*, Sports Economics, Management and Policy 17, https://doi.org/10.1007/978-3-030-52340-4_4

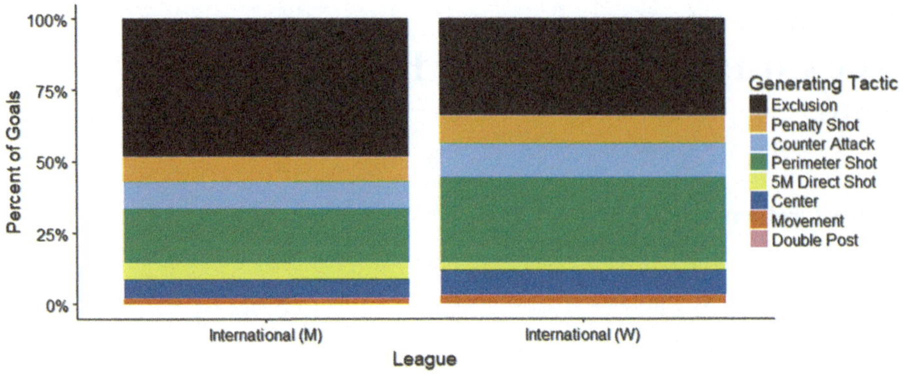

Fig. 4.1 Breakdown of goal-generating scenarios and tactics for 176 (97 men, 78 women) elite water polo contests FROM 2012 TO 2015. For more details on the dataset, see section "Model Description and Parameters"

men's water polo (and almost half of all goals in women's) result directly from major defensive fouls, which can take on one of two forms in the sport:

1. *Exclusions* in which a player on the defensive team is temporarily suspended for 20 seconds, giving the offense a six on five "power play" advantage, or.
2. *Penalty Shots* in which a severe goal-preventing infraction is committed within five meters of the goal, resulting in a penalty shot at the goal.

Both exclusions and penalty shots provide the offense with significant advantages and hence, any biases in the rates at which they are called could largely affect the outcomes of games.

A second reason for studying water polo officiating stems from the following paradox first pointed out in Graham and Mayberry (2014): although most goals result from major defensive fouls, the winning team rarely gets more such opportunities. Figure 4.2 shows the percentage of games in which the winning team received more scoring opportunities from defensive fouls as opposed to games in which the losing team had more opportunities. In men's contests, the winning team had more opportunities in only 37% of all contests, while in women's, they had more opportunities in only 27%. In contrast, Graham and Mayberry (2014) showed that if one looks at *Exclusion Conversion Rate*, defined as the fraction of power play opportunities, which are converted to goals, the winning team had a higher value in almost 90% of all contests, even if we restrict our attention to "close" games (those decided by 3 or fewer goals). These results again highlight the importance of exclusion opportunities while also providing evidence of a foul calling bias in favor of losing teams.

Graham and Mayberry (2016) further studied this phenomenon in elite men's water polo on a possession-by-possession basis. They defined two new statistics: the *Defensive Foul Rate* (DFR), defined as the probability of being awarded an exclusion or penalty shot opportunity on a given offensive possession, and the *Offensive*

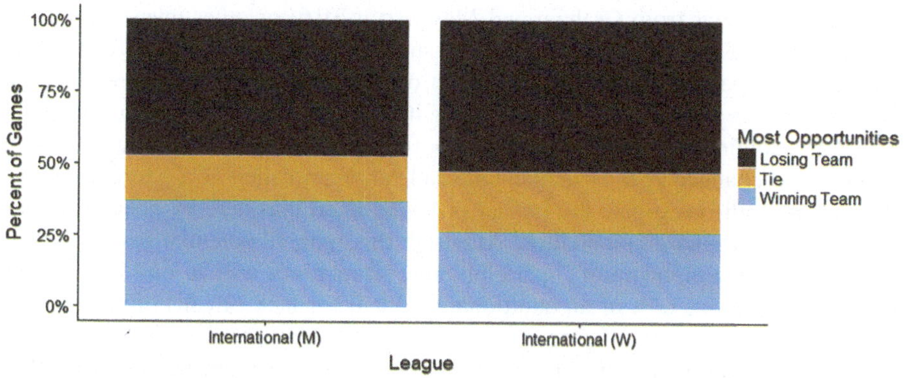

Fig. 4.2 Distribution of which team had the most scoring opportunities from defensive fouls based on the game outcome. Here tie could mean either that both teams received the same number of opportunities or that the game ended in a tie (shootouts excluded)

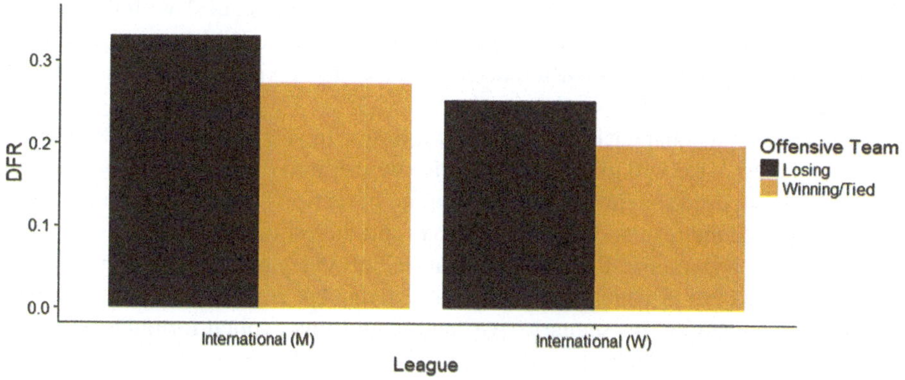

Fig. 4.3 Differences in the probabilities of the offensive team drawing a defensive foul (DFR) between losing and winning/tied teams

Foul Rate (OFR), the probability of being called for an offensive foul resulting in a turnover of possession to the opposing team. Using hierarchical logistic regression, they studied the impact of various game state factors (e.g., sign and magnitude of offensive team's lead, sequential fouls, scoring momentum) on both the DFR and OFR. In particular, they showed that there is statistically significant evidence of losing team bias in water polo officiating with the odds of drawing a major defensive foul decreasing by about 27% when the offensive team is winning or the game is tied. They also showed that this losing team bias persists even after accounting for differences in playing style (i.e., selection of offensive and defensive tactics), game-score (close vs. unbalanced games), event (Olympics, World Championships, European Championships), team, and game-time. Figure 4.3 illustrates the overall losing team bias in defensive foul calling rates.

What is unclear from Graham and Mayberry (2016) or other investigations of foul calling biases is the extent to which such biases may actually influence the outcome of a game. Evaluating the impact of losing team bias in real water polo contests is more challenging than validating its existence. It is difficult to isolate the effect of a single foul call on the outcome of a game and predict how the outcome would have changed if a particular foul had not been called at a particular time. Instead, we will investigate the impact of losing team bias here by generating our own games via random simulation. Although this ignores potential psychological effects on "game momentum'," parallel game simulations will at least allow us to assess the objective cost of an additional foul call (or lack of call) on the games' final score.

To explain our approach, imagine a contest between two equally matched elite men's teams that we will refer to as "Dark" and "White". In the real world, these two teams would only be able to play once, but in the virtual world, we can generate two parallel games, which are identical in all respects except that in Game 1, there is no losing team bias in foul calling, while in Game 2, the losing team bias is present. By comparing the pattern of goals scored by Dark in Game 1 with the pattern of goals scored by Dark in Game 2 (and similarly, compare White scoring patterns between the two games), any differences will be goals scored (or lost) as a result of losing team bias.

The rest of this chapter is organized as follows. In section "Model Description and Parameters", we will give a more precise description of our simulation process and the data set used for calibrating parameters. In section "Simulation Results", we will summarize the results of our simulations and the estimated cost of losing team bias. Section "Symmetric Bias Approximation" provides a more in-depth study of the symmetric case in which the losing team advantage is the same as the winning team disadvantage. In this scenario, we can obtain some explicit formulas based on the use of binomial probabilities. Finally, we conclude in section "Discussion" with some remarks and questions for further investigations.

Model Description and Parameters

To simulate the cost of referee bias, we generate $M = 10{,}000$ coupled pairs of games, one of which incorporates a losing team bias in foul calling and one in which foul calling rates are independent of the game-state. The evolution of each game is based on a discrete time Markov chain model in which each step represents a change in possession. A *possession* is defined as the period from when a particular team takes offensive control of the ball until offensive control returns to the opposing team. This possession-oriented approach to studying water polo was first proposed in Graham and Mayberry (2014) inspired by a similar approach earlier applied to model basketball games (Kubatko et al. 2007).

The state of the unbiased game during game possession k is a triple (D_k, W_k, O_k) where D_k, W_k tracks the current game score and O_k tracks who is currently in possession of the ball. During each possession, a goal is scored with probability g independent of the current score. Possession then switches to the opposing team and the process continues for N possessions where N is a random variable. The team who gets the ball first is determined by a fair coin flip. The unbiased game is then "coupled" with the biased game in the following way:

- If the offensive team is losing during possession k, then a goal is scored in both games with probability g and only in the biased game with probability b_ℓ for some parameter $b_\ell > 0$.
- If the offensive team is winning or the game is tied during possession k, then a goal is scored in both games with probability $g - b_w$ and only in the unbiased game with probability b_w for some parameter $b_w > 0$.

The parameters b_ℓ, b_w represent the respective boost and reduction in goal-scoring rates, resulting from losing team bias.

To determine appropriate values for the parameters g, b_w, b_ℓ and the distribution of N, we used game data from 68 elite men's water polo games including 23 from the 2012 London Olympics (henceforth Oly), 25 from the 2013 World Championships (WC), and 20 from the 2014 European Chamionships (EC)[1]. This data set included all playoff games from the three tournaments as well as selected games from the preliminary rounds between competitive teams. The teams involved in these games are listed in Table 4.1. Games were filmed from midcourt by representatives from Team USA water polo. While camera position varied, all twelve players and the defending goalie were kept in frame at all times. The first author or one of his assistants later viewed the recorded tapes and play-by-play game logs were recorded summarizing the outcomes of all possessions in the contests. Information transcribed about the possession included the team on offense, offensive tactic(s) employed[2], any defensive fouls called, rebounds/new clocks, and the ultimate result of the possession (Goal, Missed Shot, Blocked Shot, Goalie Save, Turnover, or Offensive Foul).

Overall, our data set included 4625 possessions (1556 from Oly, 1766 from WC, and 1303 from EC). The distribution for the number of possessions per game was roughly symmetric (median = 68, mean = 68.9 possessions per game) with 50% of all games having between 65 and 73 possessions and 90% of all games having between 60 and 76.7 possessions. Figure 4.4 shows the distribution of possessions across games and this empirical distribution was used to bootstrap sample N in our simulations.

---

[1]The figures in Section 1 also included 29 men's games from various 2015 international tournaments and world qualifiers, but these were excluded from our model because of slight differences in tracking methods and the competitiveness of the events. We also excluded women's games from our model because of differences in game play and foul calling rates. Building a similar model for women's water polo would be an interesting project for future investigations although a complication is that winnings/tied teams tend to score nonexclusion goals at a higher rate than losing teams and hence, the model assumptions used here would be invalid.

[2]See Graham and Mayberry (2014) for a further discussion of offensive tactic classifications.

Table 4.1 Teams involved in our dataset

Team	Number of games
AUS	11
CAN	2
CHN	3
CRO	15
ESP	14
GER	2
GRE	13
HUN	16
ITA	15
MNE	14
ROM	1
ROU	7
SRB	15
USA	8

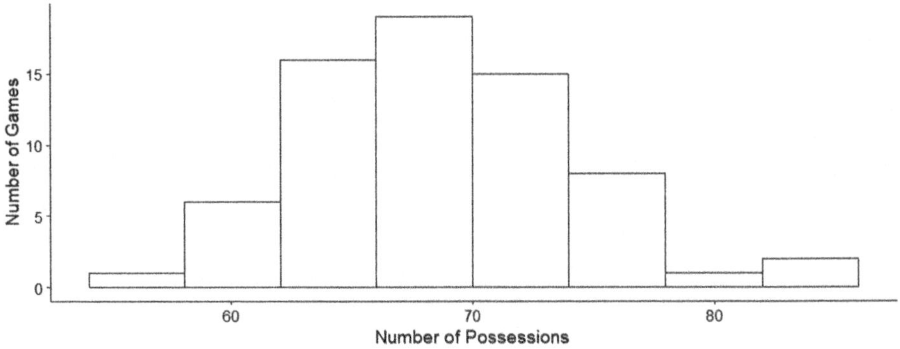

Fig. 4.4 Distribution of number of possessions per game

To determine the goal-scoring probability g and the losing team bias, we categorized possessions according to the following four scenarios:

- G: A goal was scored with no foul being called.
- P: A single penalty shot was granted, resulting from a severe goal-preventing infraction.
- E: An exclusion foul was called, resulting in a 20 second 6 on 5 power play advantage for the offense.
- C: A change of possession occurred without any of the three above outcomes. Change of possession could mean a turnover, blocked shot, saved shot, missed shot, offensive foul, or shot clock violation.

Table 4.2 Percentage of possessions ending in each of the four possible outcomes G,P,E,C based on the starting state of the possession with respect to the offensive team

Offense	Count	G	P	E	C
L	1888	0.106	0.018	0.326	0.550
W/T	2800	0.109	0.019	0.257	0.615
Overall	4688	0.108	0.019	0.285	0.589

L = Offensive team losing, W/T = Offensive team winning or tied

Table 4.3 Defensive Foul Statistics including mean number of fouls per game (Mean), conversion rates (CR), and margin of error in conversion rate estimates at a 95% confidence level (ME)

Type	Mean	CR	ME
Exclusion	20.7	0.46	0.03
Penalty shot	1.3	0.75	0.11

Table 4.2 summarizes the fraction of each possession ending in each outcome broken down by the offensive state at the start of the possession (offensive team losing or winning/tied).

We estimate the probability g of scoring a goal in a given possession by taking a weighted average of the three outcomes that could result in a goal:

$$g = G_O + \varepsilon E_O + \rho P_{O,}$$

where G_O, E_O, P_O are the overall fractions of possessions resulting in G, E, P and ε, ρ are the exclusion and penalty conversion rates, respectively. Estimates of ε and ρ from our database are provided in Table 4.3. Finally, we estimate the foul calling biases b_w, b_ℓ by the formulas:

$$b_w = \left(E_O - E_{WT}\right) \times \varepsilon,$$

$$b_\ell = \left(E_L - E_O\right) \times \varepsilon,$$

where E_{WT} and E_ℓ are the probabilities of drawing an exclusion when the offensive team is winning/tied or losing, respectively. Since the goal-scoring and penalty shot rates did not differ significantly between losing and winning/tied teams, we leave these factors identical in the biased and unbiased games. Therefore, the winning and losing team goal-scoring biases depend only on differences in exclusion calling rates between the two scenarios.

Simulation Results

We employ two metrics to quantify the impact of losing team bias in our simulations:

1. *Difference in goals scored*: defined as the difference between the total numbers of goals scored in the biased game and the total number of goals scored in the unbiased games.
2. *Alteration of Final Outcome*: defined as a binary variable that takes on the value of 1 if the outcome of the biased game differed from the outcome of the unbiased game. This includes situations in which one game was tied and the other yielded a clear victory for one team.

We illustrate the computation of these metrics in Fig. 4.5 that shows one coupled simulation of a single game between teams Dark and White. Comparing Dark 1 (the goals scored by team Dark in the unbiased game) with Dark 2 (goals scored by Dark in the biased game), we can see that there are no differences until Possession 27. At this point, the Dark team is leading in both games, but due to the presence of losing team bias in Game 2, they score a goal in Game 1 and not in Game 2. During Possession 41, the Dark team is hurt again in Game 2 when the game is tied. In contrast, the White team scores lie on the same trajectory until Possession 66. At this point, the White team is leading in Game 2 and is then hurt by a losing team bias. Therefore, to summarize the impact of losing team bias in this game, we can say that it cost the Dark team two goals and cost the White team 1, changing the game outcome from a 13–12 win for Dark to an 11–11 tie. In terms of our metrics, the difference in goals scored was 3 and the alteration of outcome was 1.

Figure 4.6 shows the distribution of the difference in goals scored across all 10,000 simulated games. On average, losing team bias did not affect the total number of goals scored and approximately 48% of all simulations ended with no difference between the two games. Another 42% of all games ended with a total goal difference of 1; however, the symmetry of the distribution implies that the total number of goals was just as likely to be higher in the biased games as in the unbiased games. There were a few outliers (like the game shown in Fig. 4.5) in which the total number of goals in the two games differed by as much as three.

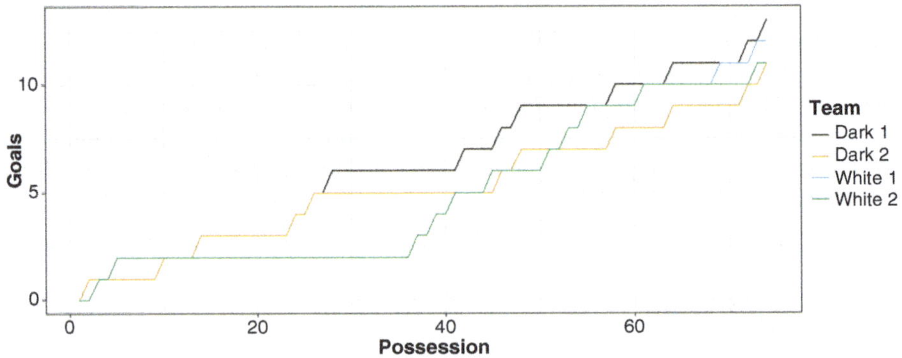

Fig. 4.5 Sample of a coupled game simulation demonstrating the difference between the biased (Dark 2 vs White 2) and unbiased (Dark 1 vs White 1) games

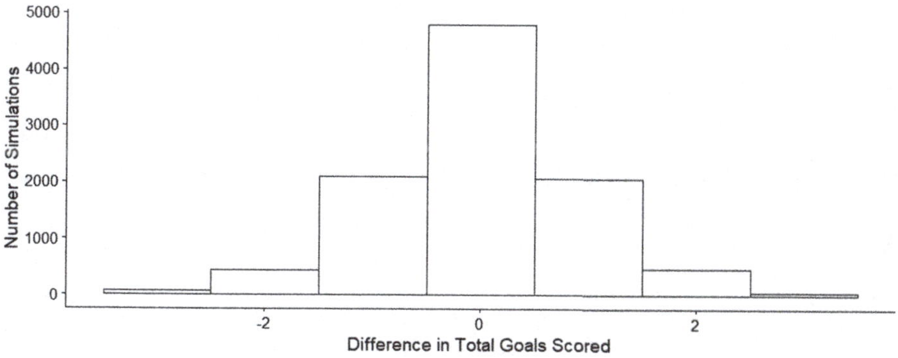

Fig. 4.6 Histogram showing the distribution of the difference in goals scored across all 10,000 simulated games in our sample

Fig. 4.7 Distribution of game alterations

In contrast to Fig. 4.6, Fig. 4.7 shows the impact of losing team bias on game outcome in our database. Overall, about 14% of all game outcomes were altered by the presence of losing team bias. The most common alteration was from a clear victory for one team in the unbiased game to a tie in the biased game. Only 1.3% of all alterations actually switched the winner of the game from Dark to White (or vice versa).

Symmetric Bias Approximation

To demonstrate the sensitivity of our simulation results to parameter selection, we include a discussion of how the fraction f of all games altered changes as a function of the amount of bias present in a game. For simplicity, we restrict our attention to the sym-

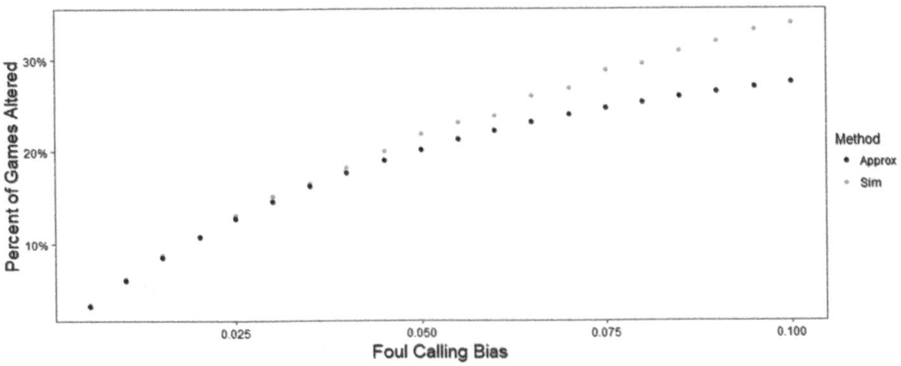

Fig. 4.8 Comparison of symmetric bias with theoretical approximations

metric case where the boost in foul calling biases for the losing team is equal to the reduction in foul calling rates for winning/tied teams. Figure 4.8 shows the results of 10,000 simulated games at various foul calling biases, ranging from 0.005 to 0.1. From Table 4.2, we can see that the foul calling bias in men's water polo is not quite symmetric: losing teams get a boost in exclusion calling rates of around 0.041 per possession, while winning/tied teams get a reduction of only 0.028. Nevertheless, using a symmetric bias of between 0.03 and 0.04 provides a rough approximation to this scenario.

Figure 4.8 shows the results of these simulations. When the foul calling bias is small, the shape of this curve can be explained by direct computation. During each possession, the probability of a goal being scored in one game but not the other is $b_w = b_\ell = b$. Therefore, the probability of at least one extra goal being scored in the biased game is

$$1-(1-b)^n$$

Of course, this is not enough to actually change the outcome of a game, but when b is small, the probability of more than one extra goal being scored is relatively small and hence, most game-altering situations will fall into one of the following two categories:

3. The unbiased games ends in a tie, but one team scores at least one extra goal in the biased game.
4. The unbiased game score differential is 1, but the losing team scores at least one extra goal in the biased game.

Since goal-scoring events are independent, the final scores in the unbiased game can be approximated by independent binomial random variables D and W, each with approximately $\nu/2$ trials and success probability g where ν is the mean number of possessions per game. Therefore, the probability of scenario 1 above is approximately

$$P(D=W)\times\left(1-(1-b)^{\nu}\right)$$

and the probability of 2 is

$$P(\|D-W\|=1)\times\left(1-\left(1-b\right)^{\frac{v}{2}}\right).$$

Therefore, we can approximate the fraction $f(b)$ of altered games as

$$f(b)\approx P(D=W)\times\left(1-(1-b)^{v}\right)+P(\|D-W\|=1)\times\left(1-(1-b)^{v/2}\right).$$

ν can be computed from the data (see section "Model Description and Parameters" and Fig. 4.4), while from standard formulas for Binomial probabilities, we can easily compute

$$P(D=W)=\sum_{j=0}^{v/2}\left[\binom{v/2}{j}g^{j}\left(1-g\right)^{v/2-j}\right]^{2}$$

and

$$P(\|D-W\|=1)=\sum_{j=0}^{\frac{v}{2}}\binom{\frac{v}{2}}{j}g^{j}\left(1-g\right)^{\frac{v}{2}-j}\times\left[\binom{\frac{v}{2}}{j-1}g^{j-1}\left(1-g\right)^{\frac{v}{2}-j+1}+\binom{\frac{v}{2}}{j+1}g^{j+1}\left(1-g\right)^{\frac{v}{2}-j-1}\right].$$

The resulting approximation is shown in Fig. 4.8 along with the simulated values, and we see it provides a good approximation for foul calling biases of 0.05 or smaller, which contains the case of international men's water polo[3]. For larger b, the approximation is invalid, because it ignores the now relevant percentage of all games, which differ by more than one goal in the unbiased scenario as well as the games in which both teams could have received multiple offsetting calls in the biased game.

Discussion

Parallel game simulations provide a novel approach for investigating the impact of foul calling biases. By running a game twice, once with and once without a particular type of bias, we can isolate the impact of this factor on the evolution of the game.

[3] In international women's water polo, the foul calling bias is smaller, ranging from a 0.03 boost for losing teams to a 0.02 reduction for winning/tied teams.

Here, we focus on losing team bias, the established fact that a losing team in water polo has a better chance of getting a foul call in their favor than the winning team. Our simulations suggest that the presence of this bias will alter the total number of goals scored in about half of all games between typical, equally matched elite teams and could be altering the outcome in about 14% of all such games. A small fraction (just over 1%) of these alterations actually switched the winner of the contest, but the most common alteration was switching from a clear victory for one team in the independent game to a tie in the biased game. This means that the main effect of losing team bias is producing more overtime games than there should be. We also were able to examine the dependence of the fraction of games altered on the size of the losing team bias, which may help understand the impact in leagues where the amount of bias is stronger (or less strong) than in elite men's water polo.

One improvement that could be made to our simulations is in the method by which game length was determined. We determined game length at the start of a simulation by randomly sampling a value from the empirical distribution of possessions and then running the game. However, in reality, the number of possessions is also impacted by the number of exclusion fouls called, since such fouls add to the length of a possession. A more robust model would be to give a fixed game time and allow possession lengths to vary according to a random variable with additional time added after each called exclusion. Unfortunately, our data set does not provide information on the length of possessions, so we were unable to compare how this alteration would affect our results. Another improvement that could be made to our simulations is the inclusion of other factors that have been shown to affect foul calling rates such as sequential foul call biasing.

In Graham and Mayberry (2016), it is shown that losing team bias is present more strongly in close games than blowouts and persists across different offensive and defensive tactical choices. Here, we also show that the direct goal-scoring rates for losing and winning teams are similar (see Table 4.2) and that the differences in foul calling rates feed into differences in turnover rates. Together, these results suggest that referee decisions influence losing team bias in foul calls more than team performance or tactical decisions. This analysis does not address whether or not the referees benefit from this behavior. However, these observations are consistent with an old adage that referees prefer to be "fair" (giving equal opportunities to both teams) as opposed to being "objective" (calling fouls based on severity of infractions alone) (Askins 1978). With the help of parallel simulations, we have provided evidence that this principle is affecting a significant fraction of games and generating more excitement (or anxiety) than otherwise would be the case in elite international water polo.

References

Anderson, K. J., & Pierce, D. A. (2009). Officiating bias: The effect of foul differential on foul calls in NCAA basketball. *Journal of Sports Sciences, 27*(7), 687–694. Routledge.

Askins, R. L. (1978). The official reacting to pressure. *Referee, 3*, 17–20.

Brymer, R., Holcomb, T. R., & Rodenberg, R. M. (2015). Referee analytics: Bias in major college football officiating. In *2015 Mit Sloan sports analytics conference*.

Graham, J., & Mayberry, J. (2014). Measures of tactical efficiency in water polo. *Journal of Quantitative Analysis in Sports, 10*(1), 67–79.

Graham, J., & Mayberry, J. (2016). The ebb and flow of official calls in water polo. *Journal of Sports Analytics, 2*(2), 61–71. IOS Press.

Green, E., & Daniels, D. P. (2014). What does it take to call a strike? Three biases in umpire decision making. In *2014 Mit Sloan Sports Analytics Conference*.

Kubatko, J., Oliver, D., Pelton, K., & Rosenbaum, D. T. (2007). A starting point for analyzing basketball statistics. *Journal of Quantitative Analysis in Sports, 3*, 3.

Moskowitz, T., & Wertheim, L. J. (2012). *Scorecasting: The hidden influences behind how sports are played and games are won*. Three Rivers Press.

Nevill, A. M., & Holder, R. L. (1999). Home advantage in sport. *Sports Medicine, 28*(4), 221–236. Springer.

Noecker, C. A., & Roback, P. (2012). New insights on the tendency of NCAA basketball officials to even out foul calls. *Journal of Quantitative Analysis in Sports, 8*, 3.

Plessner, H., & Betsch, T. (2001). Sequential effects in important referee decisions: The case of penalties in soccer. *Journal of Sport and Exercise Psychology, 23*(3), 254–259.

Chapter 5
A Tale of Two Continents: Why Do Eastern European Males and American Females Excel at Water Polo?

Jill S. Harris

Without both genes and environments, there are not outcomes.
—David Epstein

Abstract In the sport of water polo, taller players are better offensively and defensively. A survey of the dominant male and female Olympic teams reveals that the best male players come from and play for Eastern Europe and the best female players tend to come from or play for the United States. In both cases, the question of access to the sport is pivotal. A brief history of the development of water polo is included.

Hungarian fans chanted "*Hajra Magyarok*! (Go Hungarians!)" as blood poured from the gaping wound over Ervin Zador's eye. Just minutes before Hungary defeated the Soviet Union in the semifinal match, a Soviet player smacked Zador in the face—just across his brow bone. This was 1956: the Melbourne Olympics. Tensions were unusually high in this game. Global politics were working themselves out in the pool like a prickly offense. Even though more than a decade had passed since the end of World War II, the shifting geopolitical landscape created an intense rivalry between the two countries. It was probably inevitable that the players came to blows.

The injured Zador stood victorious with the Hungarian team on the medal podium in spite of the fact he could not play in the gold medal match. It would not be the last time Hungarians bowed their heads to receive medals from Olympic hosts. Hungary dominates men's Olympic polo with nine gold medal wins, three silver finishes, and three bronze. To this day, Hungarian, Croatian, and Serbian

J. S. Harris (✉)
United States Air Force Academy, Colorado Springs, CO, USA
e-mail: jill.harris@afacademy.af.edu

J. S. Harris (ed.), *The Economics of Aquatic Sports*, Sports Economics, Management and Policy 17, https://doi.org/10.1007/978-3-030-52340-4_5

players are highly prized.[1] It could be that Eastern Europeans are simply gritty; they can take a punch from the opposing team and keep on playing. But, are there other attributes that makes them powerhouses in the pool?

Water polo athletes are basically playing rugby in the water. The sport is part swim and part basketball, and part wrestling and part baseball. Players must be able to sprint back and forth across the length of the 20 to 30 meter pool. Once they set up an offense, they must be able to tread water and fight off defenders who can press them—especially if they have the ball. Imagine this: could you wrestle a 200-pound defender while treading water and trying to pass the ball or shoot it toward a goal? The best water polo players will have something in common with the best swimmers, wrestlers, basketball players, and baseball players. Height is key—particularly in goalies who need to fill the cage and block attempted shots. Wingspan is also desirable. But, good lung capacity and strong legs are equally vital to all players when defending one-one-one.

Of course, all of this is wasted if a player cannot shoot the water polo ball with speed and precision into the goal. The best players, then, will have the speed of a competitive swimmer, the stamina and agility of a wrestler, the sensibilities of a basketball player, and the arm of a pitcher. Hungary, Croatia, and Serbia do not necessarily produce top athletes in these sports. But, they do produce champion water polo players. To help us understand why, it is useful to visit the work of David Epstein (2014), Stephen Jay Gould (1988), and Bejan et al. (2010).

Epstein writes about what he calls the "sports gene." In his chapter titled "The Big Bang of Body Types," Epstein reports that tall athletes have grown taller than nonathletes as a whole and smaller athletes have become—well—smaller. He reports something quite remarkable:

> Measurements of elite Croatian water polo players from 1980 to 1998 show that over two decades, the players' arm lengths increased more than an inch, five times as much as those of the Croatian population during the same period.[2]

He also notes that Hungarian males have broader wingspans for their height than other males. Other researchers tell the same story.[3] This one feature of Croat and Hungarian physiology may go a long way toward explaining the allure of the Eastern European player in US pools. In Hungary, competition for the tall athlete is lackluster. If you grow up big and tall in Texas, you are likely going to be recruited by the local football coach. Not so in Hungary. Maybe the local football (soccer) team will try to get you, but it is more than likely the water polo program already had you in the water before you were in high school. Long time Stanford Water Polo Coach

[1]The USC Trojan Men's Roster for 2017 includes Marin Dasic from Croatia, Mihajlo Milicevic from Belgrade, Serbia, and Lazar Pauljevic from Herceg Novi, Montenegro. The NCAA reports that 16 male Serbian players, four Hungarians and four Montenegrans are on Water Polo rosters this year.

[2]Epstein (2014), p. 118.

[3]See Lozovina and Pavicic (2004). https://www.ncbi.nlm.nih.gov/pubmed/15103759

Dante Dettamanti explains why this is true.[4] He explains that the average height of the 2012 Gold medal Croatian men's team was 6′5″ and all players were over 6′3″.

In contrast, the average height of the 2012 US Olympic team was 6′4"and all players were over 6′1″—an important difference. Beyond pure height, wingspan matters more than ever as the game emphasizes shooting over a defender, steals and the "whipping motion" required to shoot effectively. Merrill Moses, the goalkeeper on the US Men's team, has a wingspan of 6′8″ relative to his 6′3″ of height. Coaches are asking for (and expecting) this in their top players.

That explains part of the dominance of Hungarian, Croatian, and Montenegran men. People from Eastern Europe are among tallest in the world.[5] Table 5.1 reports on the top nine countries with the tallest men in comparison to the United States.

Males from Eastern Europe are two to three inches taller than American males on average. It is not unusual to see floating goals in the open water of the Adriatic Sea along the coast of Croatia and Montenegro. Hungary is land-locked. But, basketball, football, and baseball are not competing for athletes in Hungary. Therefore, water polo can still draw from the best pool of athletes.

The story changes, however, when we turn our attention to the women's Olympic game. The US Women won gold in Rio in 2016 and London in 2012. They earned silver in 2008, bronze in 2004, and silver in 2000. The US Women's team has outperformed the US men's team certainly. Yet, these female athletes obviously did not grow up in Eastern Europe. Table 5.2 lists where the tallest females, on average, come from.[6]

Table 5.1 Where the tallest males come from?

Country	Height in meters	Height in feet
Netherlands	1.83	6′0"
Montenegro	1.83	6′0"
Denmark	1.83	6′0"
Norway	1.82	5′11.75"
Serbia	1.824	5′11.5"
	1.81	5′11.25"
Croatia	1.805	5′11"
Czech Republic	1.803	5′11"
Slovenia	1.803	5′11"
United States	1.763	5′9.5"

[4] Dante Dettamanti is the Stanford University Water Polo Coach. These comments are taken from an interview on www.waterpoloplanet.com accessed 2/9/2018.

[5] This list is taken from http://www.averageheight.co accessed 02/09/18 and corroborated by a study from Imperial College London https://elifesciences.org/articles/13410 accessed0 6/18/18.

[6] This list is taken from http://www.averageheight.co accessed 02/09/18 and corroborated by a study from Imperial College London https://elifesciences.org/articles/13410 accessed0 6/18/18.

Table 5.2 Where the tallest females come from?

Country	Height in meters	Height in feet
Latvia	1.699	5′7"
Netherlands	1.699	5′7"
Denmark	1.687	5′6.5"
Lithuania	1.675	5′6"
Belarus	1.675	5′6"
Czech Republic	1.672	5′5.75"
Slovakia	1.656	5′5.25"
Estonia	1.65	5′5"
Serbia	1.638	5′4.5"
United States	1.622	5′3.75"

On average, women from the United States are almost four inches shorter than the tallest women hailing from—Eastern Europe. Yet, the average height of the Women's 2012 Olympic Gold medal squad is 5′10″, whereas the average height of the silver medal Spaniards is 5′9″. So, why would men's Olympic water polo be dominated by players from Eastern Europe, but the women's game be dominated by Americans? Especially when the average height of women in the United States is considerably less than that of women from Eastern Europe?

One reason is access. The Ligue Europeenne de Natation (LEN) for Women began play in 1987, while the men's water polo league had a 23-year head start. We suspect this has more to do with access to collegiate sport participation (something we will take up in Chap. 6 in more detail). European players good enough to play professionally will go directly into the numerous professional European leagues (like the LEN). However, the good, but not great, players have no place to go to continue playing the sport. These players come to the United States and play for the NCAA. European athletes do not have access to a collegiate league to hone their skills. The NCAA experience is quite attractive to an athlete who still wants to develop in the sport. On top of athletics, the athlete has educational opportunities that surpass what is offered in their home country. What's not to like?

This leads to the second reason. In the United States, Title IX legislation made it easier for female athletes to compete in high school and college sports alike. In 1972, Congress enacted Title IX as part of several education amendments that had a legal compliance timeline of 1978 for all public institutions. Title IX mandated, "No person in the United States shall, on the basis of sex, be excluded from participation in, be denied the benefits of, or be subjected to discrimination under any education program or activity receiving Federal financial assistance" (Bell 2007). Once Title IX compliance took root, it opened the doors for thousands more female athletes in the United States. Participation rates increased. For example, in 1981, the number of female athletes in the NCAA was 74,239 compared to 169,800 males. By 2016, that number had increased to a total of 214,086 women compared to 278,445 men (Irick 2015).

Given the population of the United States is, in many cases, hundreds of times larger than that of its Olympic competitors, it is not surprising that the pool of female athletes—short and tall—is much larger than other country's pools. Thus, the United States ends up with a women's water polo team that is taller, stronger, and more dominant.

This argument would not surprise evolutionary biologist, Stephan Jay Gould. His work shows up quite a few places in the economics of sport literature—for good reason.[7] Gould observes that the distribution of talent in a population will compress as the number of participants in a sport increases. If you imagine that the distribution of athletic talent in a population is normal, it would look something like Fig. 5.1.

Gould's notion is that the right-hand tail of the distribution is limited by biomechanics. If the population is very large, there will be many more athletes in the most talented pool than if the population is small. When the population is small, athletes of average talent may be more "competitive" in a given sport simply because fewer athletes exist in the right-hand tail.

Thus, in a country where the population of tall female athletes is small, there will be fewer very talented tall athletes in the right-hand tail. This could partially explain why the European female Olympic squads are a full inch shorter than the Americans. The population of tall female athletes is larger in America compared to Spain or Australia (even though the average height of women is much smaller).

In research that is a close cousin of Gould's, Bejan et al. (2010) suggest that the center of gravity is different for athletes of different races. In particular, they report that anthropometric literature shows the center of mass is three percent higher in blacks than in whites. Their works shows that this differential gives black athletes a 1.5 percent advantage in speed in running. When it comes to water sports (where the advantage is gained by the upper body rising above the water), this physiological difference gives white athletes a 1.5 percent speed advantage in swimming. This would also create an advantage for water polo players.

Bejan, an engineer, found in prior work that this feature helps to explain speed differentials in animals and can also potentially explain differences in other species.

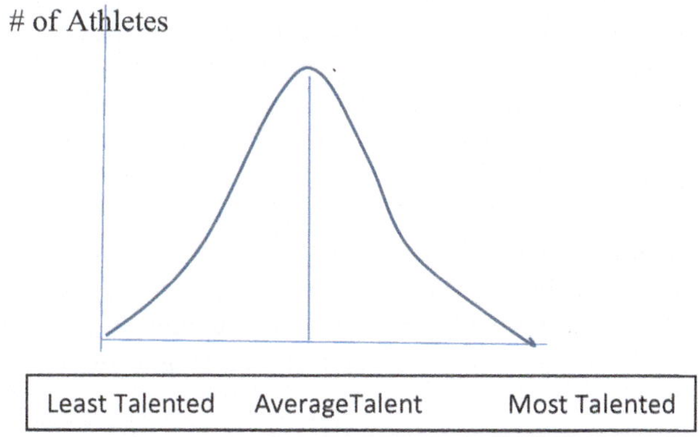

Fig. 5.1 The distribution of athletic talent

[7] See Berri et al. (2005), for example.

Their research is unique in that it "...is to study phenotypic (somatotropin) differences of human locomotion in different media (terrestrial vs. aquatic), which we consider to have been historically misclassified as racial characteristics)." [Bejan et al. 2010 p 199] They point to a wide phenotypic and genotypic diversity within the "so-called" racial types to validate their approach. The team modeled the human body as a cylinder and compared these cylinders to animal studies to calibrate what they call "falling-forward locomotion."

In swimmers, the falling-forward motion is likened to a seesaw activity. Swimmers with longer arms create more displacement so that they end up falling forward faster in the water. This means that swimmers with a lower center of body mass should have the speed advantage. It also suggests that water polo players with wingspans greater than their height will have the advantage in the water.

Several studies confirm anthropometric measurements differ systematically among blacks, whites, and Asians.[8] For men of the same height, Asians tend to have the tallest sitting height (compared to Whites and Blacks). This all interleaves with the center of gravity hypothesis. Asians have longer relative torsos. But, when it comes to speed, the absolutely longer torsos will still dominate. In women's swim, Asian athletes compete well, because, overall, the distribution of height is not as spread out. However, the authors predict this will eventually change as female elite swimmers get taller. The authors show that these records are correlated with an increase in body mass and height.

When Zador's eye was healing up from the 1956 Olympic game, water polo in Hungary was already a premier sport. When Zador defected to the United States, modern competitive water polo was in its infancy. There were no serious feeder programs, no strong collegiate programs, and, therefore, no Olympians in the USA. It would take a couple more decades for the Americans to catch up.

USA Water Polo, the national governing body for the sport in the United States, was formed in 1978. It was a volunteer organization for decades. By 2006, USA Water Polo had evolved to its sophisticated business model in line with guidance from the Olympic Committee. Today, there are nearly 500 "high-performance" club programs around the country with over 45,000 participants annually.[9] In 2009, USA Water Polo launched an Olympic Development program. Roughly 3500 athletes participate in this key pipeline experience. Together with the elite program, Splashball programs were introduced the same year. US Women's participation rates are skyrocketing, thanks to the back-to-back Gold Medal performances of the US Olympic squad.

Somewhere in the intersection of these three ideas (increased participation due to Title IX, the compression of talent as the population increases, and anthropometric differentiation) we may find the reason Ervin Zador—and the American women—was/are so good at water polo. On the one hand, a country's geography, demography, and access to markets for water polo make the biggest impact on the quantity

---

[8] See Hime (1988), for example.

[9] http://www.usawaterpolo.org/about-us/history.html accessed 2/13/2018

and quality of players coming from its borders. On the other hand, institutional change (via Title IX) tips the scales in favor of the country with the most access to participation.

References

Bejan, A., Jones, E. C., & Charles, J. D. (2010). The evolution of speed in athletics: why the fastest runners are black and swimmers white. *International Journal of Design & Nature and Ecodynamics, 5*(3), 199–211.

Bell, R. C. (2007). A history of women in sport prior to Title IX. *The Sport Journal, 10*, 2.

Berri, D. J., Brook, S. L., Frick, B., Fenn, A. J., & Vicente-Mayoral, R. (2005). The short supply of tall people: competitive imbalance and the National Basketball Association. *Journal of Economic Issues, 39*(4), 1029–1041.

Epstein, D. (2014). *The sports gene: Inside the science of extraordinary athletic performance*. London, England. Penguin Books.

Gould, S. J. (1988). Trends as changes in variance: a new slant on progress and directionality in evolution. *Journal of Paleontology, 62*(3), 319–329.

Hime, J. H. (1988). Racial variation in physique and body composition. *Canadian Journal of Sport Science, 13*(2), 117–126.

Irick, E. (2015). *NCAA report on student athlete participation. NCAA reports*. http://www.ncaa-publications.com/productdownloads/PR1516.pdf. Accessed 06/05/2018.

Lozovina, V., & Pavicic, L. (2004). Anthropometric changes in elite male water polo players: survey in 1980 and 1995. *Croatian Medical Journal, 45*(2), 202–205.

Part II
Economics of Elite Swimming

Chapter 6
Blocked Entry and Demand Shocks in Age-Group and Collegiate Swimming

Jill S. Harris and Claudia Ferrante

> *I want to be an inspiration, but I would like there to be a day when it is not 'Simone the black swimmer.'*
>
> —Simone Manuel

Abstract A labor-leisure model helps explain why entry into competitive swim is blocked. Swim has been, historically, a racially uniform sport. Demand shocks during Olympic years may portend that a different era is coming. Blocked entry is related to competitive balance in the sport. A Hirschman-Hirfindahl index of competitive balance in collegiate swim is used to compare swim to other sports.

A third grader perches on the starting block waiting for the referee's whistle. Her goggles are set-checked twice in the last 10 seconds. A parent crouches at the opposite end of the pool: her phone is ready to capture every stroke and flip turn. The typical age-group swimmer might swim in four or five events at a meet. The meet will start early in the morning (say, seven o'clock) and may run until dinnertime. Swim meets are labor-intensive experiences. Parents spend hours of waiting around for mere minutes of competition (sometimes mere seconds of competition if it is a sprint event). As children age up and compete at the high school or Junior Olympic (JO) level, our dutiful parent is getting up at four o'clock in the morning to take the child to morning practice before school, three to five mornings a week. These are in addition to regular after-school practices.

Swim competition is unique—not only in its practice regimen—but in its execution as well. Consider the setup for a typical meet. The races are organized into heats: usually three heats (there can be more depending on the number of swimmers in the meet). Slower swimmers swim first; the fastest swims occur in the last heat.

J. S. Harris (✉) · C. Ferrante
United States Air Force Academy, Colorado Springs, CO, USA
e-mail: jill.harris@afacademy.af.edu

J. S. Harris (ed.), *The Economics of Aquatic Sports*, Sports Economics, Management and Policy 17, https://doi.org/10.1007/978-3-030-52340-4_6

The athletes may specialize later on in their swim careers, but starting out, they probably swim all strokes: freestyle, back, breast, and butterfly. Then, there are the medley races and relay races. Meets require hundreds of volunteer hours. Set up, take down, timers, officials, heat posters, results posters. Again, all of this labor to support races that only last a minute or two; most, last just a few seconds. The longest swims (500 meters) can take up to five or six minutes. The 50-meter sprints take less than 30 seconds.

Because of the hefty time commitment from families and the high price for club dues, competitive swim at the collegiate and national levels suffers from a blocked entry problem. With few exceptions, its superstars come from families with two parents in the home and above-average household incomes. Generally, these families are Caucasian. Time spent on a pool deck is time not spent working at an hourly job. Of course, there are exceptions. Michael Phelps was raised by a single parent—his mother. However, she was a middle-school teacher and principal in Towson, Maryland. Towson's median household income is $77,680 and principal salaries in that area of the country are in excess of $100,000. [1]

Another exception is Simone Manuel: the first African-American to win a gold medal in an individual swimming event. Her background, though, still helps to make the case that entry into swimming is blocked. Manuel grew up in Sugar Land, Texas. She attended Stephen F. Austin High School in Fort Bend County Texas outside of Houston.[2] This area has median household incomes far above the national average. In fact, by race, the African-American householders in this area have estimated median incomes of $89,000, according to census tract data from 2012–2016. Manuel's brothers participated in a summer swim program, so she followed suit. The Manuel family lives in an area where swim programs are abundant and families earn income sufficient to afford swimming "consumption." However, it is less likely we would have watched Manuel earn a gold medal if her family had hailed from, say, Del Rio, Texas, instead of Sugarland. Del Rio has a median household income of $41,110 per year.

The social history of swim in the United States is chaotic.[3] According to Wilste (2007), access to public and private pools was historically restricted on racial lines. This cultural phenomenon prevented generations of would-be athletes from entering the water and competing in the sport. Even if families had the financial means to place their child in age-group swim programs, it is clear they hesitated to do so. Desegregation, then integration, of public swimming pools was disorderly. This led to the rise in development of private swimming, which further restricted assess of nonwhites to swimming and, therefore, water polo and aquatic sports in general.

Anecdotal stories from black aquatic athletes support Mr. Wiltse's analysis. If athletes in your neighborhood all play basketball or run track and field, swimming and water polo would be foreign to you. An interview in USA Water Polo provides

[1] https://www1.salary.com/MD/School-Principal-salary.html accessed 06/19/18.

[2] https://en.wikipedia.org/wiki/Simone_Manuel accessed on June 19, 2018.

[3] The discussion of racism and swimming is based largely on Wiltse (2007).

some examples.[4] The article highlights Ashleigh Johnson, arguably the best female water polo goalie in the world, and Mia Rycraw, an Arizona State goalkeeper. Both of these female athletes are African-Americans. Szabo reports that both Johnson and Rycraw marveled at the adversity they encountered from minority and nonminority athletes. Other minority athletes question why they did not play basketball or other "neighborhood" sports. Many comment they never knew water polo existed and wonder how a black athlete plays it at all. Access to pools and programs is obviously one important key to participation in the sport. For many families, access to swim programs is blocked.

A simple choice model can help to partially explain the blocked access. Laborers have 24 hours of labor or leisure each day, 168 hours each week. A household (or parent) can devote all 168 hours to labor if they needed no sleep or all 168 hours to leisure. If too much leisure is consumed, the household may not have enough income earned from labor to buy groceries or pay the rent. Of course, what is more reasonable is that the household decides to allocate some hours to both.

Theory suggests the trade-off between all other goods and leisure may be affected by the total amount of income a laborer has in her budget constraint. That is, the choices I make about the number of hours I work if I am making $20,000 a year may be different than the choices I make if I am making $120,000 a year. This means that with a lower income, less leisure is consumed and, by default, more labor is consumed.

When we apply this model to the decision to "consume" swim competitions in the household consumption bundle, it is easy to see that laborers earning more income will choose more leisure than those with a less income. This simple insight helps us understand one aspect of the consumption of swim competition state-by-state. Consider Table 6.1, which shows the median income for the neighborhoods of the top six competitive swimmers, top six female soccer players, and top six male soccer players in 2017. In addition, it shows the total number of "learn-to" programs in each sport in these areas and the average cost of participation.

Although the average number of "learn-to" programs is the same in this small sample, the average median incomes from the athlete hometown neighborhoods are not. The deviation from the state median income is 1.82 times larger for swim households than soccer households. Swim fees are monthly and reflect year-round instruction. Soccer requires a one-time registration fee for programming that is three times a week for three months on average. Swim participation is roughly five times more expensive. Of course, there may be many other variables influencing the family's (and athlete's) choice of sport. But, this comparison supports the blocked entry story: Swimming is a relatively more expensive sport than soccer. Swimmers tend to come from higher-income areas and/or higher-income families. So, not only are the explicit costs of participation higher in swim, the implicit costs are high as well. The fee and time costs comprise a larger share of time and money for

[4] Matt Szabo wrote for USA Water Polo www.usawaterpolo.org/genrel/081717aaa.html accessed 2/9/2018

Table 6.1 Median income for athlete hometowns (compared to state median income)

Swim	Neighborhood	Median income	Programs
Chase Kalisz	Bel Air, MD	$91,824 $69,272 MD	7 swim $110/mo 4 soccer $80 reg.
Simone Manuel	Sugarland, TX	$89,000 $53,000 TX	30 swim $90/mo 0 soccer
Lilly King	Evansville, IN	$52,000 $53,314 IN	4 swim $70/mo 0 soccer
Katie Ledecky	Bethseda, MD	$168,000 $69,272 MD	64 swim 128/mo 5 soccer $175 reg.
Caeleb Dressel	Green Cove Springs, FL	$68,000 $44,250 FL	8 swim $103/mo 0 soccer
Matt Grevers	Lake Forest, IL	$155,000 $60,960 IL	33 soccer $75 reg 25 swim $100/mo
Soccer Alex Morgan	Diamond Bar, CA	$106,000 $67,739 CA	117 soccer $125 reg 25 swim $115/mo
Samantha Mewis	Weymouth, MA	$86,000 $75,297 MA	2 soccer $95 reg 21 swim $120/mo
Julie Ertz	Mesa, AZ	$64,000 $48,621 AZ	9 soccer $95 reg 7 swim $75/mo
Christian Pulisic	Hershey, PA	$59,000 $56,907 PA	21 soccer $85 reg 10 swim $100/mo
Michael Bradley	Pennington, NJ	$117,000 $71,637 NJ	7 soccer $85 reg 12 swim $110/mo
Jozy Altidore	Boca Raton, FL	$73,000 $44,250 FL	12 soccer $150 reg 20 swim $100/mo
Average Swim		**$103,970**	**18.41 $101.75/mo**
Average Soccer		**$68,166**	**17.5 $80.40 registration**

Table 6.1 shows the median income from each athlete's high school or hometown. It also shows the number of AYSO soccer clubs and USA Swim Clubs and the average fees in the surrounding 30-mile area for comparison. Median income figures are from US Census Bureau data

low-income families than for high-income families. This is true if we assume that lower-income families must choose consumption bundles that have less leisure in them.

Demand shocks during Olympic years

It appears that competitive and age-group swimming experience demand shocks on an Olympic cycle. We see this trend twice nationally after Phelps' record-breaking Olympic performances and once on a state-wide level in Colorado after Missy Franklin earned gold at the 2012 games at the age of 17. After Phelps' 2008 performance, age-group swimming increased by 2.48 million participants.[5] Then, after his London 2012 performance, another 1.44 million swimmers got in the pool nationwide.

The effect from Missy Franklin is perhaps less predictable but more interesting. Post Franklin's London 2012 performance, Colorado Swimming (Franklin's home state at the time) saw a 14 percent increase in 2013 and USA Swim participation grew 13 percent. There is a construction boom in swim facilities in Colorado. Clubs have long waitlists and are turning away swimmers because they do not have room.

Franklin was born in Pasadena, California, but grew up in Centennial Colorado. She attended Regis Jesuit High School in Aurora Colorado and graduated in 2013. Franklin joined the Colorado Stars Travel (coached by Todd Schmitz) swim team at 7 years old. By the time she was 13, she swam in the 2008 Olympic Team Trials. She did not qualify that year, but the experience prepared her to ultimately make the team for the 2012 London games. She won four gold medals in London and, in total, she owns 27 medals in international competition.

Before 2012, there were 12 total USA swim programs in Colorado. Put differently, post the Olympics and Franklin's performance, there are 38 USA swim programs in the Denver metroplex (Denver population is 682,545) and 30 programs within Colorado Springs. All programs are at capacity. For the first time in Colorado's history, developers are building pools. To put these numbers in perspective, the city of San Diego, California, has a population of 1.41 million people. It has 21 USA swim team programs. For a sense of how many swimmers these programs support, in 2004, there were 4561 year-round swimmers registered in Colorado. In 2014, that number ballooned to 7173.

So, there are more age-group swimmers—arguably as a result of the superstar performances of Phelps and Franklin. One might think that the pool of elite athletes would be larger as a result. However, this is not the case. Even if you have more athletes entering the pipeline, the crowd thins quite a bit once swimmers graduate high school. If you do not have JO (Junior Olympic) or Olympic qualifying times, it is difficult to go to college on a swim scholarship.

Six hundred sixty four schools sponsored varsity swimming and diving teams in 2017. In NCAA Division I, there are 133 men's teams and 195 women's teams. The average team size is 28 swimmers. There is a limit of nine scholarships for men and 14 for women. This means that with 28 male swimmers, and a limit of nine scholarships, each swimmer may only have about one-third of the cost of college covered. This would be true only if the school fully funds swim. There were 138,364 US high school swimmers in 2016–2017. There are 10,823 college swimmers. This translates to 2.5% of US High School swimmers competing at NCAA D1 Schools.[6]

Where do the nation's top high school swimmers choose to go to college? Table 6.2 shows where the top 20 swimmers (in terms of Olympic medals) went to college.

[5] According to the Outdoor Foundation based on a sample of 12,631 household surveys in 2018.

[6] http://www.scholarshipstats.com/swimming.htm accessed 1/17/2018.

Table 6.2 Top 20 swimmers and colleges attended

Swimmer	School	Years
Michael Phelps	Univ. Michigan	2003–2007
Mark Spitz	Indiana	1964–1968
Matt Biondi	Cal Berkeley	1984–1988
Jenny Thompson	Stanford	1991–1995
Ryan Lochte	Univ. Florida	2003–2007
Amy Van Dyken	Univ. Arizona Colorado State Univ.	1991–1995
Gary Hall Jr	Univ. Texas	1992–1996
Katie Ledecky	Stanford	2016–
Aaron Perisol	Univ. Texas Austin	2002–2006
Nathan Adrian	Cal Berkeley	2006–2010
Tom Jager	UCLA	1982–1986
Don Schollander	Yale	1964–1968
Dara Torres	Univ. Florida	1985–1990
Jason Lezak	UCSB	1993–1997
Matt Grevers	Northwestern	2003–2007
Allison Schmitt	Univ. Georgia	2009–2013
Natalie Coughlin	Cal Berkeley	2001–2005 U
Shirley Babashoff Amanda Beard Charles Daniels	n/a Univ. of Arizona n/a	1976 1998–2002 1908

Cal Berkeley has a slight edge with three of the top Olympians, while Stanford, the University of Texas, and the University of Arizona each can claim two. If we consider the all-time Olympic-production totals for the top schools, the results are different: Cal Berkeley has produced 85 total Olympians, Stanford produced 79 Olympians, Michigan produced 78, and the University of Texas produced 72. The case of the University of Florida is interesting. Eighty-eight swim Olympians have emerged from the Gator system; however, 55 of those 88 swam for other countries. Which program produces the best swimmers? In spite of the fact that Michigan launched the most famous swimmer in the world, it only has one in the top 20. Berkeley, on the other hand, launched 85 total Olympians and has three on the top 20 list. Arguably, the best swimmers go to and come from the University of California Berkeley.

Olympic Dreams

If you are lucky enough to be in the 2.5% of high school swimmers that go on to swim in D1 programs, you have a better chance than other aquatic athletes to compete in the Olympic Games. Table 6.3 shows the breakdown of college athletes in aquatic sports for the 2016 Rio Games.

Table 6.3 College athletes at the 2016 olympics

Sport	Number of athletes	M	F
Swim	45	23	22
Water Polo	10	3	7
Diving	6	2	4

Number of college athletes on aquatic teams for the 2016 Rio Olympics

Stanford sent the most current student-athletes to Rio (29 athletes). Of the 555 American athletes on the Olympic squad in 2016, 417 were incoming, current, or former NCAA student athletes. Swimmers are roughly eight percent of the total team and 11 percent of the student athlete population at the games.

Overall, the road to the Olympic Games for swimmers is quite narrow. An athlete, generally, must begin an age-group year round swim program by age seven or eight. The athlete must be fast enough to qualify for the Junior Olympics and be lucky enough to receive a berth with 2.5% of the total high school swimmers that are recruited to swim for D1 programs nationally (about 3459 swimmers). Finally, to qualify for the Olympics, you must be in the top one percent of collegiate athletes.

A single swim family can invest thousands of hours for this one percent chance. If that family cannot "afford" the time sacrifice, the third grader on the starting block will never be the Medalist on the Olympic block.

Competitive Balance

Given the blocked entry problem and extremely tight pipeline in swim, it is natural to wonder whether the sport is competitively balanced. There are a variety of measures that gauge the concentration of wins in a sport. Some look at within-season variations; some consider between-season variations. Still others examine championships won over a period of time. This is the measure we will employ.

Table 6.4 lists the Division I swim, football, and basketball championships for 20 years of competition. Italicized names indicate consecutive championships, while bold names indicate championships across more than one sport. A Hirschman-Hirfindahl index (HHI) of concentration is estimated for each sport. This was done by squaring the ratio of championships won divided by years under consideration by each school, and then summing the results. The higher the number, the more concentrated the league.

Men's swim is the least competitively balanced by championship, while football is the most competitively balanced during this time period. Men's swim also has the most "streakiness" in terms of back-to-back championships. Stanford, California, and Texas are "streaky" schools. This is not surprising given our earlier discussion of the Olympic production these schools create. What is surprising, perhaps, is the presence of Auburn on the men's side and Georgia on the women's side. These schools have not produced as many Olympians (Auburn has produced 43 Olympians

Table 6.4 Division I swim, football and basketball champions

Swim M	Swim W	Football	Basketball M	Basketball W
2018 Texas	*Stanford*	(none)	Villanova	Notre Dame
2017 Texas	*Stanford*	Alabama	North Carolina	South Carolina
2016 Texas	Georgia	Clemson	Villanova	*Connecticut*
2015 Texas	California	Alabama	Duke	*Connecticut*
2014 California	*Georgia*	Ohio State	**Connecticut**	***Connecticut***
2013 Michigan	*Georgia*	Florida State	Louisville	*Connecticut*
2012 California	*California*	*Alabama*	Kentucky	Baylor
2011 California	*California*	*Alabama*	Connecticut	Texas AM
2010 Texas	Florida	Auburn	Duke	*Connecticut*
2009 Auburn	California	Alabama	North Carolina	*Connecticut*
2008 Arizona	Arizona	Florida	Kansas	*Tennessee*
2007Auburn	*Auburn*	Louisiana	*Florida*	*Tennessee*
2006 Auburn	*Auburn*	**Florida**	***Florida***	Maryland
2005 Auburn	Georgia	Texas	North Carolina	Baylor
2004 Auburn	*Auburn*	USC	**Connecticut**	***Connecticut***
2003 Auburn	*Auburn*	LSU USC	Syracuse	*Connecticut*
2002 Texas	*Auburn*	Ohio State	Maryland	*Connecticut*
2001 Texas	*Georgia*	Miami (FLA)	Duke	Notre Dame
2000 Texas	*Georgia*	Oklahoma	Michigan State	Connecticut
1999 Auburn	*Georgia*	Florida State	Connecticut	Purdue
1998 Stanford	Stanford	**Tennessee**	Kentucky	***Tennessee***
1997 Auburn	USC	Michigan Neb	Arizona	*Tennessee*
1996 Texas	*Stanford*	Florida	Kentucky	*Tennessee*
1995 Michigan	*Stanford*	*Nebraska*	UCLA	Connecticut
1994 *Stanford*	*Stanford*	*Nebraska*	Arkansas	North Carolina
1993 Stanford	*Stanford*	Florida State	North Carolina	Texas Tech
1992 Stanford	***Stanford***	Alabama	*Duke*	**Stanford**
1991 Texas	*Texas*	Wash. Miami	*Duke*	Tennessee
1990 Texas	*Texas*	Colorado Georgia Tech	UNLV	Stanford
HHI = 215	HHI = 161	HHI = 76	HHI = 83	HHI = 174

Bold names indicate the college had more than one championship team that year. *Italicized names* indicate consecutive championships

and Georgia has produced 63). Yet, they clearly have dominated collegiate competition during the past 20 years.

This curiosity is explained by the rules of engagement for college swim meet competition. Swimmers who make the Olympic team do so based purely on their personal times for each event they enter. The fastest times qualify for the team. Swimmers who win collegiate swim meets do so based on a team point system for first, second, and third place finishes. First place finishes earn six points, while second place earns four points and third place earns three, fourth place earns two points, and there is one point awarded for fifth place. Thus, teams may win a swim meet without having the fastest swimmers or fastest times in any given event.

Coaches can be strategic from event to event. For example, a coach may know that she does not have the fastest time in the 200 m butterfly, but she bets they will take second and third. The team can still win the meet in this case so long as the overall point total is higher at the end. Or, suppose the opposing team has the fastest sprinters, but they are not deep in the longer races (500 meter, etc.). A winning strategy is to take one of your sprinters and throw them into the 500 meter, take your second and third place finishes in the sprints and win the meet.

We suspect (a thorough investigation may be the subject of future research) that Auburn and Georgia's programs are flush with terrific swimmers and have benefited from excellent and strategic coaching through the years. It appears, then, that swimmers may gravitate toward Auburn and Georgia if they care about winning championships. However, if they care about Olympic berths, they may gravitate toward Berkeley and the University of Texas.

It is logical to conclude that future Olympians would be clustered out of these programs and that these programs would have a recruiting advantage in subsequent years, based on the literature.[7] This feedback loop would reinforce the blocked entry problem in swim: there are four main schools that provide a direct path to an Olympic dream. If you do not make the cut, odds are you will never compete for the gold. However, if you are Michael Phelps, you defy the odds. Phelps was a freshman at the University of Michigan in 2005. At this point, he had already competed in the Sydney and Athens Olympic Games. He was the youngest male to make an Olympic squad in 68 years. He did not medal but finished fifth in the 200-meter butterfly. In Athens, he brought home six gold medals and two bronze. All of this, of course, set him up for the Beijing Olympics in 2008. But, Michigan did not take home a single championship during Phelps' college years. He was not on the roster because Phelps gave up his eligibility at age 16 when he signed on with Speedo as a professional athlete.

Back to Blocked Entry

All of this is what makes the case of Simone Manuel so fascinating. Her hometown is Sugarland, Texas—not known for turning out Olympic swimmers. She is a woman of color. She swims for Stanford. She is exceptional for her performance and for her road to the Olympics. Perhaps, her own superstar power and Olympic success will usher in a new age of swim with a more diverse group of athletes in the pipeline. Time will tell. And, just like that third grader on the starting block in her first meet of the season, these new swimmers just have to keep dropping time to make it to the next level. The future of competitive swim may indeed be more competitive in economic terms as access to pools, programs, and coaching is increased for the widest possible pool of talent.

[7] See Pope and Pope (2009, 2014), for example.

References

Pope, D. G., & Pope, J. C. (2009). The impact of college sports success on the quantity and quality of student applications. *Southern Economic Journal, 75*(3), 750–780.

Pope, D. G., & Pope, J. C. (2014). Understanding college application decisions: Why college sports success matters. *Journal of Sports Economics, 15*(2), 107–131.

Wiltse, J. (2007). *Contested waters: A social history of swimming pools in America*. Univ of North Carolina Press.

Chapter 7
Market Power, Rents, and Deadweight Welfare Loss in Collegiate Swimming

Jill S. Harris and Audrey Kline

They're not professional athletes. They're not what some people are arguing they should become, which is unionized employees of the university.

—Mark Emmert, NCAA President talking about college basketball players

Abstract As with all collegiate sports in the United States, athletes do not earn income from their labor efforts. This is due, primarily, to the structure of the NCAA as an incidental cartel. This cartel market power translates to price ceilings on wages and quotas on the number of athletes employed. On average, most college swimmers are generating at least the value of their athletic scholarship. However, some generate far more. This lays the groundwork for future work on exploitation of student-athletes and estimation of the deadweight welfare loss in aquatic sport.

The NCAA is considered an incidental cartel by most economists. Cartels are in the business of restricting output to increase revenues. Because the NCAA has exclusive control of student-athlete labor, it restricts the number of athletes that can receive scholarships to play sports for its member schools. It also sets the level and other terms of the scholarship contract. How does this allow them to earn more revenue? Athletes use their skills to produce football, basketball, and baseball games. They also use their talents to produce lacrosse, field hockey, swim, and water polo contests. At the DI level, there is a wide array of high-profile programs earning millions of dollars of revenue from these contests. Best known are the

J. S. Harris (✉)
United States Air Force Academy, Colorado Springs, CO, USA
e-mail: jill.harris@afacademy.af.edu

A. Kline
University of Louisville, Louisville, KY, USA

J. S. Harris (ed.), *The Economics of Aquatic Sports*, Sports Economics, Management and Policy 17, https://doi.org/10.1007/978-3-030-52340-4_7

spectacles produced on the gridiron; less well known are the top-tier meets and matches occurring on deck at competition pools around the country.

Of course, the revenues at the smaller schools pale in comparison to those earned by Power Five conference members, and revenues from aquatic competitions are smaller than those from football and basketball. But, the revenues generated by a top-tier swim program are larger than you might think. Aside from these "gate" revenues, top swimmers attract more applicants. Given the limited supply of swim scholarships, many of these athletes are not supported 100% and therefore pay tuition. Elite alumni help grow that organization, which creates a positive feedback loop to the admissions office and the athletic program itself. And, the same exploitation principle applies: these revenues are generated by spectators at events drawn to see outstanding student-athlete performances. The athletes do not earn any of the money. It all goes to the swim program and the NCAA [depending on broadcast rights arrangements and conference sharing arrangements]. Economic theory suggests three different ways to examine the impact of this market power in collegiate swim. We can try to estimate the rents earned by the schools from the marginal revenue products of the athletes. We can compare income shares in professional sports and, by analogy, estimate what the income share could be if athletes were allowed to be paid for their labor. Finally, we can consider the deadweight welfare loss of the quota and price ceiling effects.

Brown (1994, 2010) and Brown and Jewell (2004) develop a framework for estimating the rents earned in the college recruitment market. Brown estimates the marginal revenue product of a collegiate basketball player in two steps. First, he models the number of players drafted from a college team roster as a function of recruiting and market characteristics. Next, he regresses a team's revenues on the number of its players drafted using the fitted values from the first regression as instruments. The lower bound of these estimates from the late 1980s is just over $870,000 for a college basketball player. Updates to this approach in Brown (2011) result in estimates of over $1 million in direct revenue for a team from acquiring one more future NFL draftee. These estimated rents are clearly much higher than the average basketball or football scholarship.

Brown (2010) refers to the work of Zimbalist (2010) as a sort of robustness check. Zimbalist uses revenue shares to evaluate player compensation in Major League Baseball, the National Football League, the National Basketball Association, and the National Hockey League. He shows that roughly 60% of NFL team revenues are allocated back to players in the form of compensation. Brown computes "average" marginal revenue products and compares these to Zimbalist's 60% allocations to bolster his claim that the rents earned by college football programs are substantial.

Since college swimmers do not have the same professional opportunities as college basketball and football players, the methodology outlined above does not produce meaningful results when applied to swimming. College swimmers can compete to earn a spot on the Olympic team, however. If we model the number of Olympians selected from each program as a function of the recruiting and marketing characteristics above, then regress the college teams' revenues on the number of Olympians (using the fitted values from the first regression), the estimated coefficient on Olympians selected is 32,142.[1] This, if significant, would imply that a school earns a little over $32,000 when it recruits one more potential Olympian to its roster. Perhaps with better revenue data and a larger sample, this estimated relationship could be confirmed.

Still, there may be another way to get at the impact of collegiate market power in swimming. The "back of the envelope" method that Brown (2011) uses could be helpful in the case of swimming. Table 7.1 compares the revenues of the swim programs we profiled earlier in Chap. 6.

There are 295 reported varsity swim programs represented in Table 7.1. The total revenues reported translate into $119,495 per program, on average. However, we know some states and programs are not average. Consider the state of California in closer detail. California has 181 of the 364 swim and water polo programs. This means that each California program reported $158,742 on average. But, again, that would be a misrepresentation of the true reported revenues from the programs we are most interested in: Stanford and Cal Berkeley. Stanford reports $445,502 in revenues from their men's and women's swim programs in 2016. This is four times the average reported revenues. Cal Berkeley reports $1,746,088 in revenues for 2016 from its men's and women's teams. This is almost 11 times the average revenues.

But, what do the athletes earn? What could they earn if they were paid a professional salary? Recent work by Berri (2018) and Greer, Harris, and Berri (unpublished) examines labor's share of revenues for various professional leagues. Using this as a reasonable proxy for what amateur athletes might earn if they were allowed to be paid for their labor, they estimate player marginal revenue products and determine whether or not the athletes are exploited.[2]

Table 7.1 Reported total amount of revenues by state 2016

Varsity Sports Teams Swim	
State	Revenues
California	28,732,373
Florida	7,207,673
Georgia	2,022,425
Texas	5,533,993
Total	43,496,464

Source: U.S. Department of Education, Office of Postsecondary Education, Equity in Athletics Disclosure Act (EADA) survey

[1] This estimated coefficient is not statistically significant. As discussed in Chap. 6, many colleges do not report revenues for swimming and diving separately. And, most of the Olympic swimmers come from just a handful of NCAA DI schools. This limits the sample size and contributes to large standard errors.

[2] Exploitation is defined in the sense that Joan Robinson introduced. When a laborer earns less than her marginal revenue product, she is exploited.

The analysis is a bit trickier in swim as there is technically no professional league that organizes swim competitions. However, in the United States, USA Swim serves in this capacity. If we take 60% as a reasonable average of labor's share of revenues, then professional swimmers should earn approximately 60% of the reported revenues from USA swim.[3] As of 2017, USA Swim reported $43,631,309 in revenues. Thus, professional swimmers should earn $26,178,785 divided between them. If we use the Olympic roster for the 2016 Games, this means 45 swimmers would have theoretically earned $581,750.[4] This can be considered an upper bound of swimmer marginal revenue products.

If we apply that same 60% rule to the average revenues of all swim programs from Table 7.1, and then apply the "back of the envelope" logic from Brown (2011), we get the results in Table 7.2.

This table shows the average marginal revenue product (based on recruiting future Olympians to the roster) is $27,575. We can consider this a lower bound estimate of the average marginal revenue product for swimmers.[5] In order to check this result, let's examine the case of an Olympian from Cal Berkeley.

Cal's swim team boasts a number of Olympians. Recently, Ryan Murphy earned three gold medals in Rio. Even though we do not have the disaggregated performance and marginal productivity (yet) to establish that any of the swimmers on Cal's team are exploited, it is quite reasonable to assume that a swimmer like Ryan Murphy is. The Olympic committee paid him $25,000 for each gold medal. Over and above any "share" of league revenues, his one-time performance at one event (the Olympics) was worth $75,000. By this benchmark, we could argue that Murphy's performance at any single swim meet during his college career (where he earned a first place finish) was probably worth far more than the total $16,000 he received in the form of a scholarship *for the entire academic year.* Thus, the average marginal revenue product of $27,575 to the school for recruiting one future Olympian seems low—at least for this gold medalist.

Table 7.2 Calculation of "average" marginal revenue products

	Average team revenue to swimmers	Average future olympians	Swimmer average marginal revenue product
All Teams	$71,697	2.6	$27,575

[3]Major League Baseball labor earns 53%, National Football League Labor earns 52%, and the English Premier League earns 76%. Zimbalist (2010) estimated the NFL earns 60% of revenues.

[4]The fact that most Olympic swimmers make far less than this because of their amateur status and/or because of the inability to land the multimillion dollar contracts that Phelps, Ledecky, and Lochte have is the subject of another chapter.

[5]Again, the 2SLS approach of Brown (1994, 2011) returned an estimated coefficient on Olympian swimmers of just over $32,000; but, this result is not statistically different from zero. Still, we may want to be conservative with the lower bound estimate from the average marginal revenue product calculations in Table 7.2.

There is a third way for us to identify the effects of market power on collegiate swim. NCAA amateurism rules essentially place a price ceiling on wages for swimmers and a quota on the number of swimmers that can compete at the collegiate level. As Chap. 6 discussed, the total number of scholarships available is 9 for men and 14 for women. Yet, we know that there are over 138,000 high school swimmers—some with fast enough times to compete in Junior Olympics or Nationals. The restriction on scholarships coupled with the price ceiling creates a deadweight welfare loss (*dwl*) in the collegiate swimming market. The following equations provide two different ways to estimate this deadweight welfare loss. If we assume that NCAA DI swim programs have a perfectly elastic demand at the price ceiling (the mandated scholarship amount), then Equation 1 suggests that *dwl* can be calculated by

$$dwl = \left[\left(\overline{w} - mc\right) * \left(qt - qr\right)\right],$$

where $\left[\left(\overline{w}\right)\right]$ is the mandated scholarship amount, *mc* is the marginal cost to the school of "hiring" the swimmer, *qt* is the total unrestricted pool of potential collegiate swimmers (with competitive times), and *qr* is the restricted number of swimmers due to the quota. Using data from the EADA survey, we calculate the *dwl* as \$291,526,500.[6] Alternatively, we calculate *dwl* using the more traditional approach. If we use the average marginal revenue product from Table 7.2 as the maximum reservation price collegiate swim programs are willing to pay to hire a future Olympian, then Equation 2 suggests the *dwl* is

$$dwl = \frac{1}{2}\left[\left(\hat{w} - mc\right) * \left(qt - qr\right)\right],$$

where $\left(\hat{w}\right)$ is the maximum reservation price and all other variables are the same as Equation 1. Using the same data but with the higher wage, the *dwl* from the quota and price ceiling is \$307,713,892.

Are these estimates credible? Table 7.3 compares the calculated values from Equation 1, Equation 2, and from the price ceiling alone.

Table 7.3 Deadweight welfare loss from quota and price. Ceiling due to NCAA amateurism rules

Equation 1	\$291,526,500	$(qt–qr) = 30,687$
Equation 2	\$307,713,892	$(qt–qr) = 30,687$
Price ceiling alone	\$125,264,650	$(qt–qr) = 0$

[6]The EADA survey reports that the average cost per swimmer of a collegiate swim program is \$6500. If scholarships were not restricted about three times, the amount of high school swimmers would be competitive for college teams. Thus, (qt – qr) is estimated to be 30,687.

In 2017, the NCAA in total captured more than $1 billion in revenue.[7] Is it reasonable to assert that in one sport alone (swimming) the *dwl* from amateurism rules is a third of the cartel's total revenue? Traditionally, according to industrial organization studies, the *dwl* to the total economy of market power ranges somewhere between 6% and 10% of GDP. By that standard, these estimates are extremely high. Of course, any estimate of *dwl* is sensitive to the quantities involved in the calculation. Suppose we cut the quantities in half: the estimated dollar values are still quite staggering ($145,763,250 from Equation 1 and $161,676,686 from Equation 2). Even if we assumed that the number of swimmers stayed the same, and we simply calculate the *dwl* from the price ceiling alone, we get $125, 264,650.[8] From a philosophical standpoint, any deadweight welfare loss reduces the total surplus to society from sports production and consumption. Therefore, it seems clear that NCAA rules reduce total surplus by millions of dollars. With additional research, the scale of the loss in surplus can be refined and tested.

Studies of men's and women's basketball suggest that well over 50% of athletes in these collegiate sports are exploited—some to the tune of millions of dollars in revenue. It may not be the case that 50% of swimmers are exploited. But, the principal questions are as follows: 1) does the structure of the NCAA itself create an environment where student athletes can be exploited in swim? and 2) does the quota and artificial price ceiling create a deadweight welfare loss? The answer to both questions is yes. While not every collegiate swim program is bringing in over a million dollars, millions of dollars are at stake in the swimming industry. Katie Ledecky's decision to turn pro and give up the remaining two years of eligibility at Stanford provides evidence of this fact. Her endorsement deal with TYR is valued at $7 million. NCAA rules create deadweight welfare losses in swimming just as they do in football and basketball; they just do not get as much media attention as the revenue sports do.

References

Berri, D. J. (2018). *Sports economics*. New York: Worth Publishers.

Brown, R. W. (1994). Measuring cartel rents in the college basketball player recruitment market. *Applied Economics, 26*, 27–34.

Brown, R. W., & Jewell, R. T. (2004). Measuring marginal revenue product of college athletics: Updates estimates. In F. Rodney & F. John (Eds.), *Economics of college sports*. Westport, CT: Praeger Publishers.

Brown, R. (2010). Research note: Estimates of college football players rents. *Journal of Sports Economics, 12*(2), 200–212.

[7] As reported in https://www.usatoday.com/story/sports/college/2018/03/07/ncaa-reports-revenues-more-than-1-billion-2017/402486002/ accessed 06/19/18.

[8] The average marginal revenue product minus the average scholarship multiplied by the number of collegiate swimmers: ($25,575 – $16,000)*10,822 = $125,264,650.

Greer, T., Berri, D. J., & Harris, J. S.. (unpublished manuscript). *Exploitation in College Women's Basketball*.

U.S. Department of Education, Office of Postsecondary Education, Equity in Athletics Disclosure Act (EADA) survey

Zimbalist, A. (2010). Reflections on salary shares and salary caps. *Journal of Sports Economics, 11*, 17–28.

Chapter 8
Doping on Deck: The Prisoner's Dilemma of Performance-Enhancing Drugs

Jill S. Harris

One group of riders doped, the others alongside them racing clean. You can work out for yourselves which group was fastest.
—David Millar, Racing Through the Dark

Abstract Athletes from Olympians to NFL players are under constant pressure to be bigger, stronger, faster, and better than their competitors. Increasingly, athletes turn to Performance-Enhancing Drugs (PEDs). PEDs create a Prisoner's Dilemma within sporting organizations as athletes attempt to keep up with their opponents. This chapter addresses two questions. (1) Is doping a rational strategy and (2) Does doping provide a significant financial advantage to other clean, or nondoping, swimmers? A strategic form game indicates doping is an equilibrium strategy. Simulations from a panel data set of elite swimmers indicate the financial advantage from doping is minimal for US swimmers.

Doping scandals are so common now that we should probably stop calling them scandals and simply add the latest name to the long list of athletes who choose to take banned substances. Consider the 2018 Winter Olympics in Pyeongchang, for example. Just two weeks into the Winter Games, four athletes (a bobsledder, a curler, a hockey player, and a speed skater) failed drug tests. These athletes represented Russia, Slovenia, and Japan. They have quite a bit in common with athletes from older Olympiads. In the third Olympiad, a marathon runner, Thomas Hicks, injected himself with strychnine in the middle of the race to increase his performance. As Savulescu et al. (2004) reports, in 1976, the East German swim team won 11 out of 13 Olympic events and later claimed that the government required them to take anabolic steroids (ASs). Again, in the 2004 Olympic Games, 24 doping

J. S. Harris (✉)
United States Air Force Academy, Colorado Springs, CO, USA
e-mail: jill.harris@afacademy.af.edu

J. S. Harris (ed.), *The Economics of Aquatic Sports*, Sports Economics, Management and Policy 17, https://doi.org/10.1007/978-3-030-52340-4_8

incidents were reported (but none of these involved swimmers, divers, or water polo players).

One of the first substantial doping incidents came in the late 1980s and early 1990s when China emerged as a swimming powerhouse. In the 1988 Olympics, China only won four medals, none of which were gold. Just 6 years later at the Rome World Championships, China won 12 gold medals out of the 16 possible events. Their overall performance as a team, the masculine appearances of the athletes, and increased speed plus the reputation of the East German coaches concerned many sports leaders like Houlihan (2002). Four of the Chinese athletes tested positive for PEDs, and a month later, seven more were also found guilty of doping.

According to the International Olympic Committee (IOC), "doping" or use of PEDs is: "(1) The use of an expedient (substance or method) which is potentially harmful to athletes' health and/or capable of enhancing performance or (2) the presence in the athletes' body of a Prohibited Substance or evidence of the use of a Prohibited Method"(Maennig 2002). In order to determine if a substance is prohibited, IOC authorities ask three questions: (1) Does it enhance performance? (2) Does it have the potential to harm health? (3) Does it violate the spirt of the sport? (Irfan and Belluz 2018). The World Anti-Doping Agency (WADA) publishes a prohibited list. The list released in January 2019 details several classes of prohibitions. First, a category called substances and methods lists all the items and practices that are always illegal in and out of competition. This category includes anabolic agents, peptide hormones, human growth agents, and mimetics. Beta-2 agonists, hormone and metabolic modulators, diuretics, and masking agents are also prohibited. The categories of prohibited methods include manipulation of blood and blood components, chemical and physical manipulation of samples, and gene and cell doping. All of the above are strictly prohibited in and out of competition.

In competition, stimulants, narcotics, cannabinoids, and glucocorticoids (i.e., cortisone shots) are prohibited. Beta-blockers are prohibited in some select sports—but, not swimming.[1]

Which substances have been problematic in aquatic sport? Human growth hormone (HGH) increases muscle size and improves recovery time but does not increase the functionality of the athlete. However, there is insignificant evidence that it has increased the performance and decreased the recovery time for swimmers (Rushall and Grant 1998). By the very nature of the sport, swimming relies on overtraining, and use of HGH can increase the potential for injury. HGH can cause many side effects: injury, diabetes, heart disease, and osteoporosis (Sharma 2016).

Anabolic steroids (ASs) are synthetic derivatives of testosterone that increase protein synthesis and are typically used to increase lean muscle mass (Rushall and Grant 1998) and, therefore, AS is very popular in weightlifters and anaerobic athletes. ASs have been useful for enhancing a swimmer's strength, improving muscular endurance, increasing performance up to 400-meter swims, and decreasing

[1]The full report can be accessed here https://www.wada-ama.org/sites/default/files/wada_2019_english_prohibited_list.pdf

recovery time. Medical risks of AS include aggressiveness and possible kidney dysfunction.

The main PED used in the sport of swimming is erythropoietin (EPO) or blood doping. EPO is a natural hormone produced in the kidney that regulates red blood cell formation (Rushall and Grant 1998). Synthetic versions of EPO increase the red blood cell production to unnatural levels in order to increase oxygen within the blood stream, which increases muscular endurance. However, EPO can thicken blood, which makes the heart work harder and that can increase risk of both heart attack and stroke (Sharma 2016). Swimmers prefer this PED over most of the other drugs because it only lasts in the body for up to 24 hours, but the benefits last for 2–3 weeks. Therefore, the swimmer can use the drug, pass a drug test, and feel an increase in performance all at once.

Why is the use of PEDs controversial? For some, the basic question of fairness is the issue. Indeed, WADA's tag line is "Play True." This suggests that athletes who take banned substances or participate in prohibited methods are somehow playing "False." As Maennig (2002) outlines in *On the Economics of Doping and Corruption in International Sports*, the reason for taking prohibited substances is very similar to the reason some government officials become corrupt. Athletes that use PEDs expect to increase their expected marginal benefits to include receiving more awards, money, and endorsements. The use and success of PEDs depends on the sport and the adaptability of the athlete to different stimuli. Doping behavior is captured nicely by a strategic game form: The Prisoners' Dilemma.

In the classic Prisoners' Dilemma, two suspected criminals (let's make them drug dealers) are apprehended and held separately. There is enough credible evidence to convict the prisoners on lesser charges, but insufficient evidence to convict them both on a bigger crime. They are told that, if they confess, they will get a reduced sentence of 6 months. If one confesses and the other does not, the confessor gets set free, while the one who stays silent gets a 3-year sentence. If they both stay silent, they each serve 1-year sentence for the lesser crime. These choices and consequences can be summarized in a simple strategic game form like the one in Fig. 8.1:

What will Walter and Jesse do? The payoffs are symmetric, so both prisoners will make the same choice. If Jesse confesses while Walter stays silent, Jesse goes free. This is sounding like a good strategy so far. If Jesse confesses while Walter confesses, Jesse gets 2 years in prison. Compare those outcomes with the payoffs

Fig. 8.1 A classic prisoner's dilemma game

	Walter Silent	Walter Confess
Jesse Silent	1 year, 1 year	3 years, Set Free
Jesse Confess	Set Free, 3 years	2 years, 2 years

from Jesse staying silent. If Jesse stays silent while Walter stays silent, they both only serve a 1-year sentence. But, remember, Jesse goes free in this scenario if he confesses! Jesse will serve 3 years and Walter goes free if Jesse stays silent and Walter confesses. Given both strategies, Jesse will choose to confess. Being set free or only serving 2 years is much better than serving 1 year or 3 years. Confessing is a *dominant strategy*. Choosing to confess is best no matter what Walter does. Similarly, Walter's dominant strategy is to confess. It is the best strategy regardless of Jesse's actions.

So, Jesse and Walter both confess and serve 2 years in prison. Do you see a set of strategies that would have made them both better off? The upper left cell in Fig. 8.1 shows both prisoners only serving 1-year sentence. This is clearly a better outcome than both serving 2-year sentences! What would be necessary for Jesse and Walter to stay silent and end up with this outcome?

These types of choices occur in many strategic situations. The moral of the prisoner's dilemma is this: if you do what is in your best interest (play your dominant strategy), you may not be as well off as you could be if there were some type of agreement with the opponent. In our story, what if Jesse and Walter had a binding agreement (before their arrests) that stipulated they would both remain silent or their loved ones might be harmed? In this case, Jesse and Walter might choose to not play their dominant strategy. But, in the absence of such a credible and binding agreement, we can expect them to do what is in their own best interest. How does all of this inform our understanding of the decision by athletes to take PEDs?

In the sports world, an athlete's decision about doping can be modeled like The Prisoner's Dilemma. Consider Fig. 8.2.

Here, both the Russian and American swimmers must make a decision about their use of PEDs. The payoffs are similar but not exactly the same as those in Fig. 8.1. For both the Russian and American swimmers, staying clean would be the best outcome in terms of medals. The catch in this game is that there is no clear dominant strategy. If the Russian stays clean, she could end up with four medals or zero. If she dopes, she could end up with three medals or two. The worst outcome is if she stays clean while the American dopes. The same is true of the American swimmer.

How can we predict the outcome in a game with strategies and payoffs like this one? One way to make a prediction is to solve for an optimal mixed strategy equilibrium. If the Russian dopes one-third of the time, for example, how often should

Fig. 8.2 The decision to dope as a prisoner's dilemma

	American Clean	American Dopes
Russian Clean	4 medals, 4 medals	0 medals, 3 medals
Russian Dopes	3 medals, 0 medals	2 medals, 2 medals

the American choose to dope? Solving for the mixed strategy equilibrium requires us to set the expected outcomes (from each strategy) equal to one another. In effect, it makes each swimmer indifferent between doping and not doping.

This is done with some algebra. We want to set the expected payoff for the American swimmer from doping equal to the expected payoff from not doping. Eq. 8.1 shows the set up:

$$\rho \mathrm{Rd}(0)+(1-\rho_{Rd})(4)=\rho_{Rd}(2)+(1-\rho_{Rd})(3), \qquad (8.1)$$

where ρ is the probability that the Russian swimmer dopes and $(1-\rho)$ is the probability the swimmer does not dope. The values in the parentheses represent the payoffs for the opposing swimmer (the American in our example). In order to solve for ρ, we simply need to multiply through, collect terms, and solve for its value. The solution is

$$1=3\rho_{Rd} \text{ or } \rho_{Rd}=1/3$$

What does ρ represent? It reveals the optimal amount of times the Russian swimmer should dope in order to make the American swimmer indifferent between doping or swimming clean. In this example, the Russian chooses to dope one-third of the time. By choosing to dope often enough to make the opponent indifferent between doping and swimming clean, the Russian swimmer maximizes her returns to doping. Since the payoffs for each swimmer are symmetric, the American will choose to dope one-third of the time as well.

Simulation with US Olympic and FINA World Championships

If the mixed-strategy equilibrium suggests swimmers will dope, it might be interesting to investigate whether the decision to dope has any impact on medal earnings? Because so few dopers are caught, there is no straight-forward way to estimate this relationship with precision. However, a Monte Carlo simulation hints at the answer. We model swimmer medal earnings from a data set of 991 US Olympic and FINA World Championship swimmer year observations. Summary statistics on these data are presented in Table 8.1.

Table 8.1 Summary statistics for US Olympic and FINA championships 1982–2017

Variable	Observations	Mean	Std. Dev.	Minimum	Maximum
Gold	991	0.814	1.084	0	8
Silver	991	0.386	0.638	0	4
Bronze	991	0.226	0.495	0	3
Meet events	991	2.32	1.39	1	8

Swimmers in the sample earn more gold medals than silver or bronze medals, on average. At the elite level, swimmers specialize and swim in just a little more than 2 events per competition. In addition to these statistics, swimmers in the sample earned 803 total golds, 383 silver, and 224 bronze medals. Swimmers also qualified for 536 semifinal events and 130 preliminary events (from 1982 to 2017). At the elite level, swimmers are paid for medal performances in the Olympics and at the FINA Worlds.[2]

A linear model of swimmer earnings (as a function of performance) suggests the values reported in Table 8.2 for gold, silver, and bronze medals, respectively. The same model also suggests swimmers earn income from making it to the semifinals in any elite competition.

WADA estimates they only "catch" 1% of dopers. They also estimate that 30% to 45% of athletes take prohibited substances or participate in prohibited methods. We run the linear model 1000 times with one-third of the sample dropped each run in order to simulate a state of the world where WADA's enforcement actually captured "all" of the dopers. That is, if the dopers cannot participate in elite competitions, does compensation to the remaining swimmers change significantly? Assuming the dopers are the best performers, you might expect that if they are removed from the sample, the second best swimmers would now move up to earn more gold medals (and third best would move up to earn more silvers, etc.). If the remaining swimmers are more evenly matched, there would be fewer repeat medal performances and, as a result, earnings per gold, silver, and bronze would decrease.

Table 8.2 shows that earnings per gold medal performance decrease in the simulation. However, the simulation reveals that earnings for silver and bronze performances increase. In fact, the increased earning for bronze medal performances is $2400! Why might this be the case? If the best swimmers are being eliminated, then the remaining pool of swimmers should be more competitively balanced. And, since elimination of the best swimmers reduces gold medal-dominating performances, it stands to reason that more swimmers might earn multiple silvers and bronzes. The simulation results do not change the returns to making the semis. This makes intuitive sense as the gateway to a medal is making the semifinal rounds for all swimmers—not just dopers. Figure 8.3 summarizes the simulation results in boxplot form.

Table 8.2 Estimates of swimmer earnings from performance compared with Monte Carlo simulation results (Simulation samples 67% of existing data set with replacement)

Variable	Linear earnings model	S.E.	Monte Carlo simulation	S.E.
Gold	9892	413.20	9364	1688.65
Silver	6734	694.43	7320	2831.68
Bronze	6478	899.13	8880	3705.46
Semis	6910	2042.48	6829	5073.86

[2] The value of gold medals in the FINA Worlds over the sample period changed from $2500 to $5000, while the value of Olympic golds varied even more: from $2500 to $25,000. In the 2020 Olympics, a gold medal will be worth $37,500.

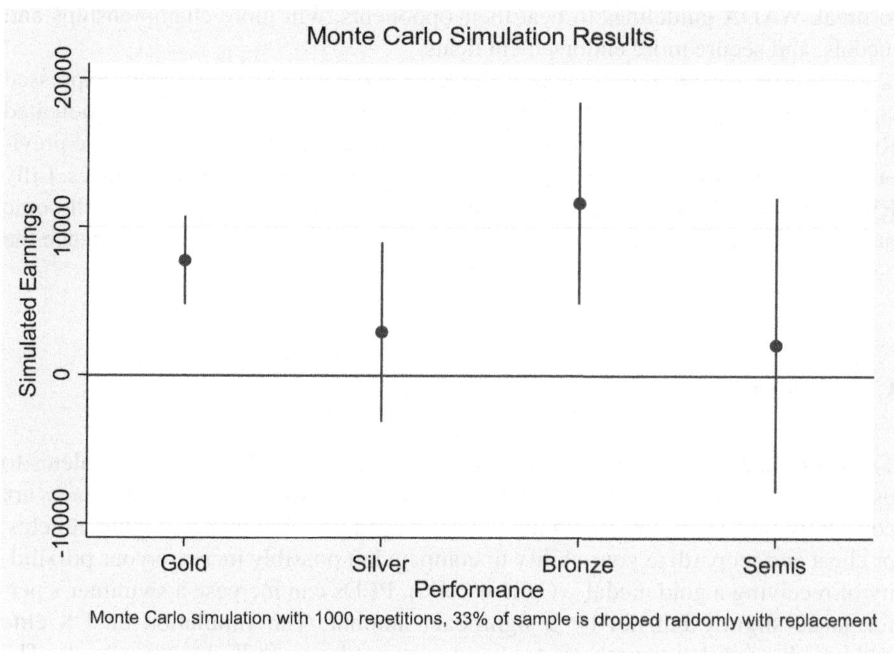

Fig. 8.3 Monte Carlo simulation results

Clearly, the simulation results are only as useful as the underlying model assumptions are reasonable. We assumed a normal distribution for the results in Table 8.2; however, changing this assumption did not change the overall pattern of simulated effects on medal earnings. The simulation hints at an answer to the question: what is the financial incentive to use PEDs or engage in prohibited methods? If we assume that at least 30% of swimmers break the rules, then total gold medal income is \$180,048 higher if the cheaters are *not* caught in a given year. This means that the lower bound of returns to cheating is approximately \$528 per gold medal performance.[3]

But, that is just the beginning. The income from earning a medal is a one-time receipt. As the next chapter shows, the real value of cheating to earn a medal is in the higher probability of signing endorsement contracts with streams of future income that can be valued in the millions. The simulation results suggest there is a positive return to doping. Still, these results cannot generalize to the total population of elite athletes that choose to dope. Since the likelihood of getting caught and punished is so low, it is a foregone Becker-type conclusion that swimmers will continue

[3]The difference between the linear model estimate of gold medal earnings and the simulation result is \$528. There are 341 unique swimmers in the panel data set \$528 multiplied by 341 yields \$180,048.

to break WADA guidelines to beat their opponents, win more championships and medals, and secure more endorsement deals.[4]

In the 2016 Rio Olympic Games, Lilly King along with Michael Phelps expressed concerns with doping at the Olympic Games. During the Games, Lilly King defeated Russia's Yulia Efimova for a gold medal in the 100-meter breaststroke. In two previous competitions, Efimova had been disqualified for use of banned substances. Lilly King spoke out after her victory saying, "...you can compete clean and still come out on top." (Jones 2016). King's defeat of a known PED-user helps to balance the perception that everyone must dope to win.

Conclusion

The continued use of PEDs in sport organizations may influence clean athletes to use these drugs in order to maintain competitiveness within the sport. Swimmers are constantly faced with this dilemma: "Play fair and possibly lose to doping athletes; or cheat and jeopardize your ability to compete but possibly increase your possibility of receiving a gold medal" (Galluzi 2000). PEDs can increase a swimmer's performance slightly but not by a significant amount. The simulation on US elite athletes showed that the returns to doping are not huge. Still, doping persists. The use of PEDs places opponents in a game similar to that of the Prisoner's Dilemma. If there is no dominant strategy, swimmers may rationally opt to use PEDs in order to remain competitive. However, the simple game may not capture or explain all athlete behavior. This is evident with Lilly King's situation; she was able to beat an individual who had a history of taking PEDs. Similarly, Tony Sharpe's sprint relay team took steroids but only took third place in the 400-meter relay. This means that two teams that (theoretically) had clean athletes were able to compete and defeat a doping team. But, this is the challenge: there is no way to know for sure if the silver and gold medal relay teams were completely clean. Until monitoring and enforcement mechanisms become more foolproof, it is very likely that doping and nondoping athletes alike will continue to step onto the medal podium in international competition—even if the returns to doping are minimal.

References

Becker, G. S. (1968). Crime and punishment: An economic approach. In *The economic dimensions of crime* (pp. 13–68). London: Palgrave Macmillan.

Galluzi, D. (2000). The doping crisis in international athletic competition: Lessons from the Chinese doping scandal in women's swimming. In Seton Hall, J., & Sport, L. (Eds), *HeinOnline*.

---

[4] Becker (1968) developed a model of crime that suggests when the returns to criminal activity are greater than the returns to legal activity, economic agents will choose crime. The probability of arrest and conviction is key parameter of the Becker model.

Houlihan, B. (2002). *Dying to win: Doping in sport and the development of anti-doping policy*. (Vol. 996). Council of Europe.

Irfan, U., & Belluz, J.. (2018, Feb 14). Four athletes tested positive for doping. It happens more than you think. *Vox*.

Jones, T.. (2016, Aug 8). Lilly King, Michael Phelps speak loudly about doping at the Olympics. *Swimming World News*.

Maennig, W. (2002, Feb). On the economics of doping and corruption in international sports. *Journal of Sports Economics, 3*(1), 61–89.

Rushall, B. S., & Grant, G. (1998). HGH, EPO, anabolic steroids, and testosterone in swimming. *Australian Swimming and Fitness, May–June, 42–44. Caringbah, New South Wales. JP Publications.*

Savulescu, J., et al. (2004, Dec 1). Why we should allow performance enhancing drugs in sport. *British Journal of Sports Medicine, British Association of Sport and Exercise Medicine, 38*(6), 666–670.

Sharma, M. (2016, July 22). How do performance-enhancing drugs affect athletes? *OUPblog, BJA Education*.

Chapter 9
The Impact of Technology and Rule Changes on Elite Swimming Performances

Todd A. McFall, Amanda L. Griffith, and Kurt W. Rotthoff

> *If you've got a spare $550, a couple of friends to zip you up, and you really need to take a second or two off your 200 butterfly time, this is the suit for you.*
>
> —Susan Casey, Sports Illustrated

Abstract We use the annual ranking of the top 100 performers in the world that the Fédération Internationale de Natation (FINA) publishes to study the impact the LZR Racer swimsuit and the deregulation of the use of dolphin kicking in breaststroke had on swimming performances. The swimsuit innovation, which was legal to use in 2008 and 2009, impacted performances across the sport such that improvement in the years swimmers could use any variation of the suit was significantly larger than in the years before it was created and after it was banned. The change in rules dictating legal motions swimmers could use while competing in breaststroke events, which occurred in 2015, caused improvement in breaststroke races to be significantly bigger than in races that involve the other strokes. We close by discussing the importance of FINA's decisions on regulating technology and monitoring innovation within the sport.

We wish to thank Chris Avallone and Sarah Peljovich for the help they provided researching this topic. We also appreciate helpful suggestions from audience members who heard variations of this chapter at the 2019 Eastern Economic Association Meetings and the 2019 Western Economic Association Meetings.

T. A. McFall (✉) · A. L. Griffith
Wake Forest University, Winston-Salem, NC, USA
e-mail: mcfallta@wfu.edu

K. W. Rotthoff
Seton Hall University, South Orange, NJ, USA

J. S. Harris (ed.), *The Economics of Aquatic Sports*, Sports Economics, Management and Policy 17, https://doi.org/10.1007/978-3-030-52340-4_9

Introduction

Economists from all branches of the discipline have been interested in better understanding the roles that technological innovations or regulatory changes have played in influencing economic growth or market outcomes. Indeed, the earliest lessons of many introductory economics classes ask students to ponder the benefits and trade-offs after innovations or regulatory changes affected various aspects of peoples' lives.

Although much of the focus of sports economics has been on the idea of competitive balance and the impact that leagues' organizational structures have on competitive outcomes, others examine the extent to which performances in sporting contests are affected by technological innovations or rule changes. In baseball, Groothuis, Rotthoff, and Strazicich (2015) examine data on player's performance for evidence of structural breaks in the way the game was played. Munasinghe, O'Flaherty, and Danninger (2001) examine the effects of globalization on performances in track and field. Finally, McFall and Treme (2012) study the way professional golfers changed their risk strategies following a rule change that outlawed the use of a particular technology used in golf club manufacturing.

We continue down the path created by these studies, as we set out to explore the implications of two exogenous shocks on performance in elite level international swimming. These shocks altered athletes' abilities to impart force and cope with the effects of friction while competing. As often happened in the past, the governors of the sport had to consider carefully the relative importance of traditions after the shocks rippled through the sport. The first shock we study is the creation of the revolutionary LZR Racer (pronounced "laser racer") in 2008. This technological marvel reduced the amount of friction that swimmers had to overcome during their races and provided additional buoyancy; this resulted in a significant boost to elite swimmers' performance times through 2009, until these full-body suits were banned in competitions. By the time the ban was in place, every world record on both the male and female sides of the ledger had been shattered, thus altering our understanding of what a truly remarkable performance is.

The other shock we study is FINA's decision to clarify the rule on the use of a dolphin kick in breaststroke events. This rule now states that an athlete can use a single underwater dolphin kick after the start and turns in breaststroke races, beginning in 2015. FINA decided to implement this rule after swimmers began using, inadvertently or otherwise, an undulating motion as part of their breaststroke pull-out (the underwater part of the stroke, where an athlete is allowed one pull and one kick before coming to the surface). Given the difficulty judges experienced monitoring athletes' underwater motions, FINA redefined the rule to allow the use of one dolphin kick, before or during the pullout (but not both), in order to ease enforcement. This kick has increased the amount of force they could exact on the water at certain moments during races. As a result of suspicious disqualifications of innocent swimmers, and missed disqualifications of guilty swimmers, FINA simply allowed the kick to occur.

We proceed by analyzing first the performance implications of the LZR Racer suit. We treat the introduction of the suit as a technological innovation and use regression techniques to measure the extent to which the suit allowed an improvement in performance times during the 2008 and 2009 seasons (the 2 years the suit was legal). We find that the suit gave female and male swimmers alike a boost in swim times, with male swimmers benefitting the most. We then analyze the breaststroke rule change by first discussing the history of the use of underwater dolphin kicking in swimming events.[1] After the deregulation occurred, swimmers could employ to their advantage the benefits of an underwater kick to lower race times. We use a difference-in-differences analysis to analyze the overall impact of the dolphin-kick rule change on swim times in the breaststroke. We find swimmers improved faster in breaststroke compared to races with other strokes since the rule change happened.

Innovation 1: The LZR Racer

In 2008, the swimming equipment manufacturer Speedo introduced its LZR Racer swimsuit. The suit revolutionized the way swimmers interacted with the water during races because of the technologically advanced material used and the innovative way the suit was constructed. Given that air is more than 750 times less dense than water, the resulting reduction in friction was exceedingly important. Plus, the additional buoyancy allowed swimmers to more easily go over the water, rather than through it, decreasing resistance. In fact, it was so successful in terms of helping swimmers push performance boundaries that FINA and the swimming world had to grapple with the question of what constitutes a proper competitive swimsuit.

As with all industries, the race for technological improvement in swimsuit technology was an industry-wide tussle, with Speedo's LZR Racer clearly winning this race in 2008. Speedo researched with NASA and university scientists various materials for constructing suits with materials that would outdo the classic LYCRA material, which constituted most competitive swimsuit designs around 2000. The aim of the research, as Tang (2008) discusses, was to find materials and new ways of constructing suits that would reduce the amount of drag swimmers presented to the water while competing. Reducing friction is critical for elite swimmers who are often separated by hundredths of seconds, which is why it is common to see swimmers wear caps to cover their hair and shave the hair from their bodies to rid the resistance the follicles create against the water.

Speedo eventually decided upon a material, LZR Pulse, that was water repellant and consisted of multiple high-density nylon and spandex weave. The fabric was not

[1] It used to be if a swimmer's hips moved at all officials called a dolphin kick, which slowly got argued that that was part of a normal pullout (if done correctly). What became hard was when they pushed the line of an undulation and a dolphin kick – which is nearly impossible to separate. Therefore, the rule applying to the dolphin kick had particular impact on these swimmers.

only lightweight, but it was highly pliable, which was important because swimmers' movements were not constricted by the use of the suit. The fabric also compressed the user's body, thereby presenting a more streamlined version of the swimmer to the water and compressing the muscles, which has been shown to increase the strength and endurance of athletes when pushing their muscles to the limit. LZR Racers would consist mostly of this fabric, which would be complemented with a polyurethane fabric at other parts of the suit. In fact, some designs of this suit would allow drag reduction over most of the suit, but increased friction in parts of the arms (allowing the athlete to pull more water with their arms, relative to a suit without it, increasing their overall propulsion).

Additionally, Speedo and its research partners rethought the way suits were constructed. Traditional suits were constructed by sewing pieces of fabric. Drag resulted from the raised fabric created by the connective stitching. Speedo used a design in which suits were made of different panels of fabric. And instead of sewing the panels together, Speedo laminated the panels in order to create a sleeker overall design that actually varied based on the event in which a swimmer competed. Thus, breaststrokers, who need to have a wide range of motion in their hips and knees, had a suit with differently situated panels compared to freestylers.

The result of these two design features was a suit that reduced drag by 38% compared to an LYCRA suit that might have been used by the generation of swimmers before the LZR Racer. The material was not only more slippery than human skin, which, for the prior generation of male swimmers, was a large part of what presented to the water in races, but the design was sleeker and provided more stability in the swimmers' core, thereby making the act of floating in the water easier than it was previously. To use economic jargon, all of these improvements added up to a world in which the marginal cost of every aspect of swimming a race fell, which meant that the amount of time it took for swimmers to complete their races would fall, too.

Immediately after the LZR Racer hit the pool decks in the summer of 2008, the swimming world had to revisit what constituted an elite performance. The technological advances were allowing second-tier swimmers to push existing world records and for top-tier swimmers to put up times that were unimaginably fast. Consider that by August 2008, once the swimming competition at the Beijing Olympics was completed, swimmers who had worn the LZR Racer had set 62 world records, 25 of which were set during the 2008 Olympic competition. (In contrast, 14 world records were set at the 2000 Olympics and eight were set during the 2004 Olympics.)

A couple of interesting and easy-to-understand data points illustrate just how revolutionary the suit was for the swimming world. First, consider that of the winning times in the 26 individual swimming races contested at the 2004 Olympics Games (held in Athens, Greece), only three would have even earned a *medal* at the Beijing Games. On the men's side, only Ian Thorpe's 200 freestyle time from the Athens Olympics, 1:44.71, would have earned any medal in Beijing in that event, such was the jump in performance across those 4 years. As for the women, only two gold-medal races in Athens would have translated to a spot on the podium in Beijing.

Chinese breaststroker Luo Xuejuan's 100 breaststroke win in Athens would have been second in Beijing, and Polish butterflyer Otylia Jedrzejczak's 200 butterfly swim would have been third in Beijing.

Along the same lines, a look at the world records (certainly the most interesting and important data points in all of the sport) reveals the extent to which the swimming world has had to wrestle with the ghost of the LZR Racer. This is especially true for men's events. Table 9.1 lists the current world records for the 26 individual events that have been contested at the Olympics since 1984.[2] The performance-enhancing role the LZR Racer played in pushing the envelope of the sport's ultimate performers is obvious. On the men's side, only six of the 16 records were set after the suit's ban in 2010. The women, on the other hand, have had an easier time outperforming the marks set in the 2008 and 2009 seasons, as only three of the 16 records set during that time have yet to be matched.

Now that we have a general idea about how potent the LZR Racer was at transforming the swimming world, we can start to think about how to measure the suit's impact in a broader, statistical sense. Improvement at the elite level of international swimming is an incremental bit-by-bit enterprise. World records fall by hundredths of a second. Many swimmers, even the world's best, improve very marginally from year to year. Facilities where swimmers perform and train improve. Slight adjustments get made to training methods that swimmers use to become faster. All of these small changes to the swimming world add up to small improvements happening year over year, resulting in performance times trending downward.

To measure this incremental improvement, and to investigate how the introduction of the LZR Racer impacted race times, we collected from the FINA website the top 100 performers in the 26 events conducted at the Olympic Games for the years 1999 to 2017. (In the five Olympics that took place in the time period our data cover, both genders' programs included the 50, 100, 200, and 400 freestyle; the 100 and 200 backstroke, breaststroke, and butterfly; and the 200 and 400 individual medley. Women competed in the 800 freestyle, while men competed in the 1500 freestyle.) This repeated cross-sectional dataset contains 49,398 observations, 24,641 of which are records of female performances and 24,757 are of male performances. We summarize the data in Table 9.2, where it can be calculated that average overall improvement of the mean time it took for males to complete their races was 3.2% in the 19 years between 1999 and 2017. The corresponding value for females was 3.1%.

The introduction of the LZR Racer creates an opportunity to test if the availability of new technology led to improvement in elite swimming in a statistical sense. We hypothesize that the technologically advanced suit allowed swimmers to improve performance times, relative to the years prior, and that this improvement should have then been removed once the ban on the suits was put in place. Therefore, we expect that while swim times were trending downward throughout the time period we study, we should see two discontinuities in this trend. First, one where

[2] At the 2020 Olympics, the men's events will include the 800-meter freestyle, while the women's events will include the 1500-meter freestyle.

Table 9.1 Men's and women's swimming world records

Men's world records				
Event	Time	Name	Nation	Date
50 m freestyle	20.91	César Cielo	Brazil	18-Dec-09
100 m freestyle	46.91	César Cielo	Brazil	30-Jul-09
200 m freestyle	1:42.00	Paul Biedermann	Germany	28-Jul-09
400 m freestyle	3:40.07	Paul Biedermann	Germany	26-Jul-09
1500 m freestyle	14:31.02	Sun Yang	China	4-Aug-12
100 m backstroke	51.85	Ryan Murphy	United States	13-Aug-16
200 m backstroke	1:51.92	Aaron Peirsol	United States	31-Jul-09
100 m breaststroke	56.88	Adam Peaty	Great Britain	21-Jul-19
200 m breaststroke	2:06.12	Anton Chupkov	Russia	21-Jul-19
100 m butterfly	49.50	Caeleb Dressel	United States	26-Jul-19
200 m butterfly	1:50.73	Kristoff Milak	Hungary	24-Jul-19
200 m individual medley	1:54.00	Ryan Lochte	United States	28-Jul-11
400 m individual medley	4:03.84	Michael Phelps	United States	10-Aug-08
4 × 100 m freestyle relay	3:08.24	United States		11-Aug-08
4 × 200 m freestyle relay	7:58.55	United States		31-Jul-09
4 × 100 m medley relay	3:27.28	United States		2-Aug-09

Women's world records				
Event	Time	Name	Nation	Date
50 m freestyle	23.67	Sarah Sjöström	Sweden	29-Jul-17
100 m freestyle	51.71	Sarah Sjöström	Sweden	23-Jul-17
200 m freestyle	1:52.98	Federica Pellegrini	Italy	29-Jul-09
400 m freestyle	3:56.46	Katie Ledecky	United States	7-Aug-16
800 m freestyle	8:04.79	Katie Ledecky	United States	12-Aug-16
1500 m freestyle	15:20.48	Katie Ledecky	United States	16-May-18
100 m backstroke	57.57	Regan Smith	United States	28-Jul-19
200 m backstroke	2:03.35	Regan Smith	United States	26-Jul-19
100 m breaststroke	1:04.13	Lilly King	United States	25-Jul-17
200 m breaststroke	2:19.11	Rikke Møller Pedersen	Denmark	1-Aug-13
100 m butterfly	55.48	Sarah Sjöström	Sweden	7-Aug-16
200 m butterfly	2:01.81	Liu Zige	China	21-Oct-09
200 m individual medley	2:06.12	Katinka Hosszú	Hungary	3-Aug-15
400 m individual medley	4:26.36	Katinka Hosszú	Hungary	6-Aug-16
4 × 100 m freestyle relay	3:30.05	Australia		5-Apr-18
4 × 200 m freestyle relay	7:41.50	Australia		25-Jul-19
4 × 100 m medley relay	3:50.40	United States		28-Jul-19

FINA lists world records are presented here: http://archives.fina.org/H2O/index.php?option=com_content&view=article&id=1271&Itemid=633

the suits were introduced, and then a second mirror-image jump when the suits were no longer allowed. Additionally, we believe that the evidence regarding men's inability to improve upon world records set during the LZR Racer relative to women's ability suggests that men received additional help from the suit, probably

Table 9.2 Descriptive statistics by gender, stroke, and distance

			Women			Men	
		1999–2017	1999	2017	1999–2017	1999	2017
Free	50 m	25.48	26.09	25.03	22.49	22.95	22.16
	100 m	55.31	56.59	54.40	49.40	50.42	48.78
	200 m	119.68	121.92	118.05	108.74	110.95	107.35
	400 m	252.06	255.72	249.55	231.51	235.55	229.10
	800 m	519.03	525.67	514.01			
	1500 m				920.91	936.77	910.23
Breast	100 m	69.22	70.98	67.86	61.64	63.15	60.31
	200 m	148.96	152.09	146.29	133.75	137.06	130.96
Fly	100 m	59.62	61.18	58.67	53.12	54.40	52.24
	200 m	131.33	133.92	129.82	118.65	120.96	116.90
Back	100 m	61.86	63.44	60.38	55.18	56.48	54.37
	200 m	132.81	135.63	130.13	120.17	122.14	118.46
IM	200 m	135.26	137.93	132.90	121.88	124.56	119.96
	400 m	285.91	290.46	281.89	252.62	265.07	257.58
	Obsons	24,641	1300	1302	24,757	1300	1301

because the difference in the amount of skin the suit covered on men was larger than the difference females experienced. So, we also hypothesize that men improved more from the use of the LZR Racer compared to women.

To accomplish these tasks, we use regression analysis, and the specification we use is shown in Eq. 9.1 below:

$$seconds_{idst} = \beta_0 + \beta_1 Male_i + \beta_2 BeforeSuit_{idst} + \beta_3 AfterSuit_{idst} + \beta_4 Year_{idst} + \gamma_d + \delta_s + \varepsilon_{idst}, \quad (9.1)$$

where $Male_i$ is an indicator variable that is set to 1 for male performances and 0 otherwise, $BeforeSuit_{idst}$ and $AfterSuit_{idst}$ are indicator variables that are set to 1 in the years before or after the suit could be used in competition, respectively, and $Year_{idst}$ is included to allow for a linear trend in performance times. The error term, ε, is assumed to be mean 0 with a variance of σ^2. Given the structure of our Eq. 9.1, if our hypothesis about the LZR Racer causing improvement in performance time is true, then the coefficient estimates on $BeforeSuit_{idst}$ and $AfterSuit_{idst}$ should be greater than 0, since the reference point of those two indicator variables is the 2 years when the suit was legal.

We show the results in Table 9.3 of the estimation from using Eq. 9.1. Note that the coefficient estimate on *BeforeSuit in* column 1 is positive and precisely estimated, indicating a roughly two second gain in average performance time with the introduction of the suit, compared to times beforehand. Contrary to our original hypothesis, the coefficient on *AfterSuit* is not statistically significant in the main model. This appears to be driven by the longer distance events (those 400 m and longer), as when we drop those events in column (2), we see results consistent with our original

Table 9.3 Impact of swimsuit rule changes on swim times

	(1)	(2)	(3)	(4)	(5)	(6)
VARIABLES	Both genders	All – short dist.	Women	Women – short dist.	Men	Men – short dist.
Male	−12.36***	−9.450***				
	[0.0828]	[0.0336]				
Before Suit	2.320***	0.940***	1.180***	0.967***	3.404***	0.871***
	[0.165]	[0.0698]	[0.128]	[0.0875]	[0.270]	[0.0729]
After Suit	−0.146	1.015***	1.509***	1.098***	−1.760***	0.969***
	[0.162]	[0.0683]	[0.125]	[0.0857]	[0.264]	[0.0714]
Year	−0.127***	−0.200***	−0.313***	−0.217***	0.0524*	−0.187***
	[0.0171]	[0.00725]	[0.0133]	[0.00909]	[0.0280]	[0.00757]
Constant	790.7***	439.9***	1167***	499.4***	829.9***	432.0***
	[34.40]	[14.56]	[26.71]	[18.26]	[56.31]	[15.21]
Observations	49,398	37,999	24,641	18,942	24,757	19,057
R-squared	0.998	0.993	0.999	0.995	0.998	0.996
Distance FE	Yes	Yes	Yes	Yes	Yes	Yes
Stroke FE	Yes	Yes	Yes	Yes	Yes	Yes

Note: Standard errors in brackets. *** $p < 0.01$, ** $p < 0.05$, * $p < 0.1$. Even numbered columns are restricted to performances on distances less than 400 m

hypothesis.[3] Swimmers experienced roughly a one second gain in short events as compared to before the suit was allowed, which disappears after the suit is banned. We also run separate regressions by gender, the results of which are shown in columns (3) through (6), with the odd-numbered columns showing results for all events for that sex, and the even-numbered columns restricting the sample to the short events. For female swimmers, we see results consistent with our original hypothesis in both columns (3) and (4). Female swimmers enjoyed roughly a one and a half second gain in performance times with the use of the LZR Racer suit, which disappeared after the suit was banned. In Column (5), we see a much larger significant positive coefficient for the *BeforeSuit* variable, indicating that male swimmers enjoyed a larger gain in performance times due to the availability of the suits, but this appears to be driven by the longer events. In Column (6), we see significant positive coefficients on *BeforeSuit* and *AfterSuit* for male swimmers, as hypothesized. The result in Column (5) for male swimmers suggests that males' performances after the suit ban (the negative coefficient for *AfterSuit*) improved more rapidly than during the years the suit was legal. This result also contradicts our hypothesis. We surmise that there may be a sharper trend in improvement for the

[3] For any readers concerned that this could be a result of a one second improvement in time meaning much more in a shorter distance race, we also estimated all of our models using the natural log of seconds as the outcome variable. When doing so, our results are qualitatively unchanged, with the swimsuit introduction leading to roughly a 1.2% decrease in race times, on average. The pattern of results following the ban of the swimsuit remains the same in the logged version of the model.

longer races (the 400 m events and the 1500-meter freestyle). Given the large amount of time it takes to swim these races (particularly the 1500 m, which takes roughly 3.5 times longer than any other race on the men's schedule), the results may be skewed. Once the longer races are removed from our regression analysis, the coefficient estimates on *BeforeSuit* and *AfterSuit* are positive and, therefore, supportive of our hypothesis about the effects the LZR Racer had on improvement. These results support our theory that performance was on average slower in the years prior and after swimmers used the suit in all its forms in competitions. However, our hypothesis that male swimmers might have enjoyed a bigger boost, due to the larger amount of body surface that could then be covered by the suits, does not appear to be supported by our results, once they are restricted to the shorter events. When we include the longer races, there is suggestive evidence that male swimmers enjoyed a larger boost in performance times as a result of the suits.

Innovation 2 – Deregulating Dolphin Kicking in Breaststroke Races

The second part of this chapter is about measuring the effect that another technological advancement – reversal of the dolphin-kick ban in breaststroke races in 2015 – had on average times posted in those races versus the rest of the competitive swimming ledger. Prior to the reversal of the ban, swimmers had been using an underwater dolphin kick for going on 30 years to some degree in races that featured the other three strokes, but controversial judging decisions forced FINA to reconsider its stance on the matter.[4] Beginning with the 2015 season, swimmers in FINA-sanctioned competitions could use dolphin kick once after a start and turn. We believe this adjustment to the rules benefited breaststrokers over swimmers in other strokes, so much so that we hypothesize that it allowed breaststrokers' performances to improve following the lift in the ban on a dolphin kick, while there should be no impact on the trend of improvement for races with other strokes. Also, swimmers' use of the kick forced FINA to consider carefully what the traditional idea of breaststroke is, similar to the way the governing body had to think about what constitutes a swimsuit once the LZR Racer was put to use.

The most famous example of using underwater dolphin kicking to help with performance is that of David Berkoff, a former Harvard University backstroker who started tinkering with the idea of kicking underwater for significant distances at the start of the race and after turns in the mid-1980s, as discussed in Mortenson (2018) and Poierer-Leroy (2015). Berkoff was a good – but not great – swimmer when he began staying underwater for much of the 100-yard (or 100-meter) backstroke races

[4] Underwater dolphin kick is considered one of the fastest ways to swim, behind freestyle, so the use of (or addition of) underwater dolphin kick is extremely beneficial to swimmers' performances.

in which he competed. He quickly rose to the top of the sport, setting world and national records and gaining a spot on the 1988 Olympic team. He left the Seoul Olympics with a silver medal in the 100-meter backstroke and a gold in the 4x100 meter medley relay. Perhaps more importantly, he was immortalized in the sport when his disruptive method of swimming backstroke became known as the "Berkoff Blastoff."

Berkoff's success made the swimming world question his strategy. Was a swimmer actually swimming backstroke when he or she stayed underwater for much of the race? To make the question even more important for the sport, other swimmers started to use the method in races that featured other strokes, most notably Olympic champion butterfliers Denis Pankratov and Misty Hymen. Instead of banning entirely the use of underwater kicking, FINA capped the use of the innovation at 15 meters from the start of a race and at the turns. Now, swimmers can take advantage of the increased speed underwater kicking provides, but they have to perform the traditional stroke for, at the minimum, 70 percent of the distance of races contested in long-course pools.

Berkoff's innovation altered the way swimmers went about training for peak performance. For the past 30 years, swimmers have become better and better at utilizing underwater dolphin kicking, and the use of the technique, at least in shorter backstroke, butterfly, and freestyle races, has become universal. The list of the best swimmers in the world during this time has increasingly overlapped with the list of the best underwater kickers who learned to use the technique fully to their advantage. The great Michael Phelps devastated his competition by staying under the water for extended distances during races, as did Olympic gold medalists and world record holders like Natalie Coughlin, Katinka Hosszú, and Ryan Lochte.

But, breaststroke was different, because swimmers were banned from using any dolphin kicks at any point in a race. Instead of staying underwater and kicking after starts and turns in order to maintain as much momentum as possible, breaststrokers were allowed to use an underwater pull and kick before they have to surface and start swimming the traditional breaststroke discipline. In order to make sure breaststrokers followed this rule, judges were placed on the deck of swimming pools, and they watched the swimmer's movements, looking for any movements that might be construed as a dolphin kick.

In the early 2000s, some breaststrokers started to push the limits of the dolphin-kick ban, especially during the underwater pull and kick phases of their races. It is almost unavoidable *not* to have one's body do some kind of dolphin-kick-like motion during the pulling portion of the underwater pull and kick. Many swimmers, understandably, tried to sneak a small dolphin kick during the pull, and some judges had to make difficult decisions regarding the legality of some swimmers' motions at very-high-profile swimming meets. Like in other sports, video replay was used to aid judges' decisions. But controversial and painful disqualifications were made or swimmers got away with breaking rules, and coaches and swimmers sought a clearer interpretation of the rules. Thus, in 2015, FINA announced that swimmers would be able to use one dolphin kick after each start and turn in races that involved breaststroke.

We see the resulting sturm und drang that accompanied interpretations of the rules as being similar to situations in which it is costly to monitor individuals' actions. The principal-agent dilemma is a long studied issue in the discipline, and the paper that perhaps adheres most closely to FINA's decision of simply allowing swimmers to partake in an action that is beneficial to them is Jensen and Meckling (1976), which states that costly monitoring means that accepting imperfect actions from managers is a profit-maximizing strategy for firms that are organized a certain way.

We also see the temptation breaststrokers faced to use an illegal maneuver as being similar to the temptation investors face to use insider trading to their advantage. The US government has created a law enforcement infrastructure to catch traders who use information to their advantage, but nonetheless, traders seek to profit from inside knowledge. Seen through this lens of inevitability, we view FINA's decision to allow dolphin kicking in breaststroke events as being similar to the strategy was analogous to the strategy advocated in Manne (1966) for policing insider trading, which was to stop policing altogether. Ultimately, FINA did give swimmers more freedom of movement so that it could avoid the high costs of policing and the controversy that accompanies it.

Once the ban was lifted, breaststroke swimmers had to determine how to use their dolphin kick; the ruling specified that it could come any time before the swimmer surfaced to begin swimming the traditional breaststroke.[5] Now, for a relatively short amount of time during a race, breaststrokers could take fuller advantage of the fact that swimmers move more efficiently while underwater than on the surface.

What sort of advantage was conferred to breaststrokers after the dolphin-kick ban was lifted? An article in *Swimming World* magazine explained the advantage in terms of the maximum speed swimmers could obtain at various junctures of a race. The portion of the race when swimmers are moving fastest is, not surprisingly, right after they dive in, when they reach a velocity of about 6 meters per second in the air and 4 meters per second in the water. After turns, swimmers can reach velocities of about 3 meters per second, a rate that falls to about 2.2 meters per second during underwater kicking and around 2.1 meters per second during surface swimming. The difference, however slight it may seem, between the last three values is where the rule change altered breaststroke performance.

During the ban, breaststrokers would have to maintain the momentum they created off the start or turn by using only the legal underwater pull and kick technique before they surfaced. The lifting of the ban gave them an extra tool, the underwater dolphin kick, to maintain poststart or postturn momentum.

Because swimmers who competed in races that featured the other strokes had been perfecting the use of underwater kicking for 25 years before the ban was lifted, we assert that the benefits from the innovation were diffused throughout the rest of the sport during the 19 years that characterizes our dataset. Breaststrokers, though,

[5] After the start and after each turn, the swimmer may take one arm stroke completely back to the legs during which the swimmer may be submerged. At any time prior to the first breaststroke kick after the start and after each turn, a single butterfly kick is permitted.

were unable to utilize the benefits of underwater kicking during this time. The lifting of the ban, thus, can be thought of as an innovation that only affects breaststroke races, in the time period for which we have data, and this difference enables us to hypothesize that in the time period after the ban was lifted, improvement in breaststroke races should have been bigger than improvement in races that did not feature breaststroke.

To test this hypothesis, we again turn to regression analysis. We use a model that enables us to use the difference-in-differences technique to test the extent to which improvement in breaststroke races has been different than improvement in non-breaststroke races. Our model is shown in Eq. 9.2 below:

$$Seconds_{idst} = \beta_0 + \beta_1 BreastStrokeAfter_{idst} + \gamma_d + \delta_s + \theta_t + Male_i + \varepsilon_{idst}, \qquad \text{(Eq. 9.2)}$$

where $BreststrokeAfter_{idst}$ is an indicator variable that is set to 1 for breaststroke races following the lifting of the ban and 0 otherwise. We include fixed effects γ_d, δ_s, and θ_t for the distance, stroke, and year in which a performance occurred. The variable $Male_i$ is an indicator that is set to 1 for races that featured men and 0 otherwise. The error term is assumed to be mean 0 with a standard deviation of σ^2.

This difference-in-differences model identifies the causal impact of the removal of the dolphin-kick ban on breaststroke event times if a few assumptions hold. First, it must be the case that the removal of the ban only impacted the breaststroke events. We argue that this is the case, and we also exclude all individual medley (IM) events (which have a breaststroke leg) to ensure that the rule change only applied to the "treated" events. Second, we assume that the breaststroke event times were trending in a similar manner to the other events prior to the rule change. In Fig. 9.1, we display the 100 m and 200 m events by sex in panels A through D. It can be seen within each distance for each gender that breaststroke performance times were trending downward in a very similar manner to the other events, prior to 2014. The figure does not show a sharp dip in breaststroke performance times in 2014, but our empirical analysis tests whether it is present.

The results of our estimation of equation (9.2) are shown in Table 9.4. Note first that the sign on the coefficient in the variable $\text{BreastStrokeAfter}_{\text{idst}}$ is less than zero (−1.009) and statistically significant at less than a 1% level. This result supports our hypothesis that performance in breaststroke should have improved more rapidly than performance in non-breaststroke races. Additionally, this result is economically significant, as it allows us to interpret that the mean performance in the 100 or 200 breaststroke improved by slightly more than one second compared to average performances in the other races in the post-ban period.

We ran the same model but separated the swimmers by gender and found that the removal of the dolphin-kick ban had a slightly larger impact on female breaststrokers than male breaststrokers (−0.986 vs. -0.8 in columns (2) and (3)). We find this result to be interesting because it suggests, perhaps, that male breaststrokers were more likely than females to use surreptitiously an illegal butterfly kick during their races prior to the lifting of the ban. Indeed, the popular press covered this possibility a full 10 years before the breaststroke rule was changed. After the men's 100 breast-

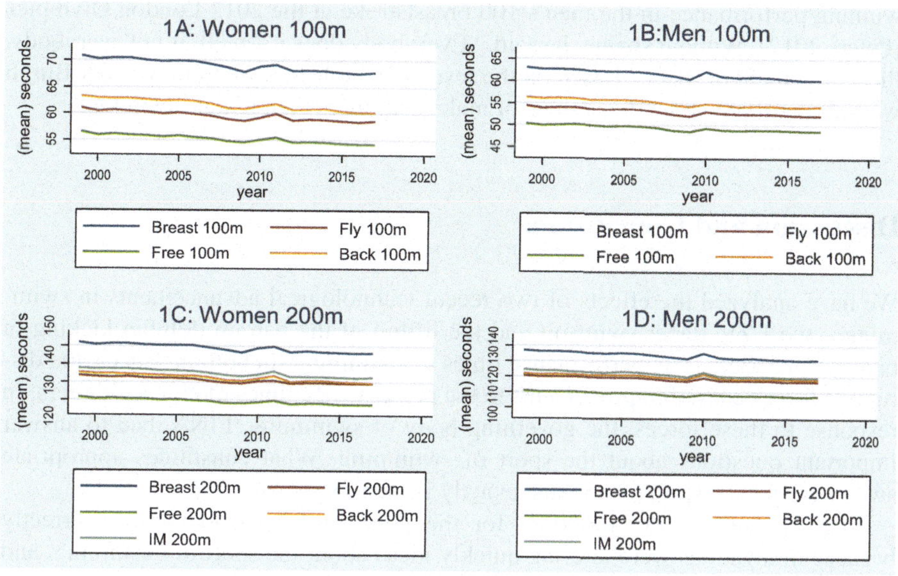

Fig. 9.1 Trends in times by gender, stroke, and distance

Table 9.4 Difference-in-differences results for impact of dolphin kick rule change in breaststroke

	(1)	(2)	(3)
VARIABLES	Both genders	Women	Men
Male	−15.19***		
	[0.0955]		
BreaststrokeAfter	−1.702***	−0.986***	−0.800***
	[0.324]	[0.239]	[0.242]
Constant	962.9***	1006***	240.4***
	[0.284]	[0.234]	[0.193]
Observations	41,988	20,239	21,749
R-squared	0.998	0.999	1.000
Distance FE	YES	YES	YES
Year FE	YES	YES	YES
Stroke FE	YES	YES	YES

Note: Standard errors in brackets. *** $p < 0.01$, ** $p < 0.05$, * $p < 0.1$. Sample excludes all individual medley events

stroke event in the 2004 Olympics, Aaron Peirsol, a prominent member of the U.S.A. team in that Olympics, loudly claimed that the event winner, Kosuke Kitajima, had used illegal dolphin kicks. About the incident, Peirsol said, "He knew what he was doing. It's cheating." The article goes on to say that Kitajima declined to comment on Peirsol's claim (Piersol 2004).

The controversy did not stop there, though. A full 8 years later, South Africa's Cameron van der Burgh admitted fully to using dolphin kicks during his gold-medal winning performance in the men's 100 breaststroke at the 2012 London Olympics (Peters 2012). Without shame, he said, "Everybody does it – well, if not everybody, then 99 percent of them." Based on the results in Table 9.4, we think van der Burgh was talking more about the actions of male swimmers than female swimmers.

Discussion and Conclusions

We have analyzed the effects of two recent technological advancements in swimming – the LZR Racer swimsuit and the lifting of the ban on dolphin kicking in breaststroke races – on performance times in swimming. In both instances, the disruptive forces caused improvements to the performance times of elite swimmers. In response to these forces, the governing body of swimming, FINA, had to answer important questions about the sport of swimming. What constitutes appropriate swimwear for the sport? And what exactly is the breaststroke?

These questions are important for the governing body to answer correctly because innovations were altering quickly ideas about the sport of swimming, and that is troubling for two reasons. The first is that a big part of the sport is the breaking of world records, which link current performances to the past. Without some type of common denominator between the past and present, the meaning and importance of those records was starting to fade, be it because of an innovative swimsuit or technique.

Remember, in 2008, swimmers set 65 world records in LZR Racers. In a typical year, there might be a handful of world records set, and the preciousness of those performances is very special to the sport, as media attention on the sport swells in these moments. But, in 2008 and 2009, there were so many world records being set that the sport lost touch with its past, because a technological advance had made swimming every race too different from the way the same races had been performed in the past.

FINA had to consider a similar dynamic when the "Berkoff Blastoff" became widely used in the early 1990s in butterfly, backstroke, and freestyle races. In a very short while, swimmers had figured out that swimming underwater was a more efficient way to swim certain races, and the sport had to consider what exactly constituted performing a stroke in a race meant, or else swimming was going to devolve into a series of underwater races with old swimming styles appearing haphazardly. And when world records fell in these events, fans and the media could have understandably scratched their heads and pondered the meaning of the feat. In a world record butterfly performance that was swum 90% underwater, was butterfly actually performed? FINA's answer to that question would define what the sport of swimming was to become after these innovations.

The link to the past that many sports celebrate is what makes sport often different from other industries. When cars usurped horse-drawn carriages as a means of transport or when email became more popular than letter writing as a form of communication, there were some people who lamented a loss to society from these new technologies. By-and-large, though, time marches on, and due to the convenience of technological innovations, we willingly decide to dissolve connections we have to the past. Sport, however, often celebrates its past because it allows for fans to understand just how great a current performer is. Baseball fans know the meaning of certain numbers like 0.376, 73, or 4256.[6] Similarly, swimming and track and field fans keep the past close at hand by taking seriously world record performances, and if swimsuits or innovative techniques alter too much fans' perception of the importance of those marks, then the sports often suffer.[7]

Ultimately, FINA decided to cap the impact of these innovations. First, underwater kicking in backstroke races was limited to 10 meters off the start and turns in 1989. Later, in the mid-1990s, the sport adopted a universal distance of 15 meters from the start and turns for nonbreaststroke events. And as we have discussed, FINA simply gave up policing dolphin kicking in breaststroke and allowed swimmers one kick off the wall in hopes to salvage the integrity of those races.

Finally, with regard to the swimsuit innovation, FINA decided to limit the amount of skin competitive swimmers could choose to cover, when it updated its rules governing swimsuit design in 2009. For females, the rules mandate currently that their necks remain uncovered and that suits do not extend past the shoulders or below the knees. For men, their option is now to cover, at most, their navel to their knees.[8] These mandates and the cap on the use of underwater kicking were both half measures that connected partially the sport to its past – after all, modern swimmers kind of dress like the old ones did and the strokes they swim have not changed – but also blessed innovations that would move the sport in unknown future directions.

References

Groothuis, P. A., Rotthoff, K. W., & Strazicich, M. C. (2015). Structural breaks in the game: The case of major league baseball. *Journal of Sports Economics, 18*(6), 622–637.

Jensen, M. C., & Meckling, W. H. (1976). Theory of the firm: Managerial behavior, agency costs, and ownership structure. *Journal of Financial Economics, 3*(4), 305–360.

Manne, H. G. (1966). *Insider trading and the stock market.* New York City: The Free Press.

McFall, T. A., & Treme, J. (2012). Pandora's groove: Analyzing the effect of the U-groove ban on PGA tour golfers' strategies and performances. *Applied Economic Letters, 8*(19), 763–768.

Mortenson, J. P. (2018, December 29). *The history of the underwater dolphin kick.* Retrieved from https://swimmingworldmagazine.com

Munasinghe, L., O'Flaherty, B., & Danninger, S. (2001). Globalization and the rate of technological progress: What track and field records show. *Journal of Political Economy, 109*(5), 1132–1149.

"Peirsol: Kitajima used illegal kick". (2004, August 15). Retrieved from https://www.espn.com

[6] Those are records for career batting average, home runs in a season, and hits in a career, respectively.

[7] Track and field was slow to use consistent policing techniques for catching users of performance-enhancing drugs, and the sport has fallen tremendously in the public consciousness since the 1980s.

[8] See the FINA guidelines on swimsuit design here: https://www.fina.org/sites/default/files/frsa.pdf

Peters, J. (2012, August 7). *The Cheatingest move in swimming: How a south African used illegal dolphin kicks to win gold*. Retrieved from https://www.slate.com.

Poirier-Leroy, O.. (2015, June 10). *David Berkoff and Daichi Suzuki's Underwater Duel in '88*. Retrieved from https://swimswam.com

Tang, K.Y. (2008, September 15). *The rocket swimsuit: Speedo's LZR racer*. Retrieved from http://sitn.hms.harvard.edu/flash/2008/issue47-2/

Chapter 10
It Is Not Easy Being Green: Gender and Earnings in Professional Swim

Jill S. Harris

I am very much looking forward to my life as a professional swimmer. I am already loving it!

—Katie Ledecky

Abstract A human capital wage model helps identify factors that influence earnings in professional swim. Females earn less than males from the sport—in spite of having more medals and slightly more endorsement contracts, on average, than the males.

Michael Phelps is the greenest swimmer ever. Not because of the famous pictures of him smoking marijuana, but because of his lifetime earnings from the sport of swim. Winning[1] 23 gold medals, three silver, and two bronze led to voluminous endorsements, which gives him an approximate net worth of $55 million. The Olympic committee awards medalists $25,000 for a gold, $15,000 for a silver, and $10,000 for a bronze. According to Money Nation, Under Armor and Visa are Phelps' largest endorsement contracts. His swim competition income is just under $2 million (career). Phelps started swimming at age seven. In 2000, at his first Olympics, he was 15 years old. At the Athens games, he won eight medals (six gold). He again won eight gold medals in Beijing. This is where the record for most golds won at a single Olympics was set. He brought home four golds from London. After Rio, Phelps broke another (ancient) record. He earned his 13th individual gold medal. The only other human to do that was Leonidas of Rhodes in 152 B.C.

[1] http://moneynation.com/michael-phelps-net-worth/ accessed 06/23/2018.

J. S. Harris (✉)
United States Air Force Academy, Colorado Springs, CO, USA
e-mail: jill.harris@afacademy.af.edu

J. S. Harris (ed.), *The Economics of Aquatic Sports*, Sports Economics, Management and Policy 17, https://doi.org/10.1007/978-3-030-52340-4_10

In addition to all those medals, Phelps owns several records. His 49.82 time still stands for the 100-meter butterfly, while his 1:51:51 owns the 200-meter butterfly record as well. In addition, his time of 4:03:84 still stands for the 400-meter Individual Medley (IM). If we break down his net worth per "medal" and "record," his performances are valued at $1.77 million each on average.

This edges out Mark Spitz's per performance value. With nine gold, one silver, and one bronze medal plus seven world records, he brings in just $1.1million for each of these accomplishments on average. The notorious Ryan Lochte's net worth is estimated to be $8 million. He has 12 Olympic medals and three standing records. This translates to $533,333 per performance. Of course, this is not the only way to consider earnings and productivity for professional swimmers. Still it offers a birds-eye-view of the money in swim… for the males. Do the females earn the same amount?

Missy Franklin's net worth is estimated to be between $2.5 and $3 million. With her five medals and three records, this puts her "per performance" value at $375,000, on average—roughly 70% of Lochte's value. Jenny Thompson earned 12 Olympic medals, just like Lochte. But, during her tenure at the top of the swimming world, her net worth was valued at just $1 million. This means her per performance value was just over $83,000, on average.

To truly determine if gender impacts earnings potential, we need to set up an empirical model of swim earnings. There are a number of these types of models in the economics of sport literature.[2] In particular, Humphreys (2000) investigates the earnings gap between male and female NCAA head basketball coaches using a human capital wage model. He finds that the gap is not attributable to the coach's gender, but instead is derived from the prestige of men's sports, fan discrimination, and the preferences of athletic directors.

Following Humphreys (2000), wages or endorsement earnings should be mostly a function of the swimmer's characteristics (age, event specialty, Olympic appearances, medals earned, gender) and possibly some fixed effects (college program). Reliable data on swimmer earnings is difficult to acquire. Many negotiations and contracts are private affairs. However, we assemble a data set including earnings, age, medal counts, Olympic appearances, event times, gender, and college programs for thirty elite swimmers (15 male and 15 female). Some of the features of this data set are summarized in Table 10.1.

Table 10.1 Summary statistics of 30 elite swimmers

Variable	Mean	Std. Dev.	Min	Max
Age	28	4.97	21	41
Gender	0.5	0.516	0	1
Medal	9.25	6.02	1	28
Oly. App	2.93	1.29	1	6
Endorsements	4	2.91	1	10
Earnings	6.8 mill.	1.38 + 07	100,000	55 mill.

[2] See Humphreys (2000), for example. Or, Simmons and Forrest (2004).

The average age (at the peak of their Olympic performances) of swimmers in our sample is 28. Dara Torres holds the distinction as the oldest Olympian in the group. She competed in her final Games at 41 years old. Half the sample is female; the average number of medals earned is just over nine. Most of the swimmers appeared in multiple Games. In terms of endorsement deals, each swimmer has about four endorsement deals on average. Michael Phelps had 10 separate contracts at his peak in the London 2012 Olympic Games. Earnings vary dramatically. The average is \$6.8 million; but, that figure is highly skewed by Phelps' earnings. His value (from endorsements) is estimated to be \$55 million. You can see, however, that the lowest earnings are \$50,000. The average earnings for female swimmers in the sample are \$975,000. For purposes of this investigation, we leave out Phelps and Ledecky as outlier observations.[3]

Equation 10.1 illustrates the basic earnings model:

$$\textbf{\textit{Earnings}}\,\textbf{\textit{S}}_{\textbf{\textit{i}}} = f\left(\begin{array}{l}\textbf{\textit{Age, Endorsement contracts, Medals, Olympic}}\\ \textbf{\textit{Appearances, Gender, College}}\end{array}\right) \tag{10.1}$$

With this model, we expect the potential impact of the explanatory variables on Swimmer i's earnings to be as follows:

- We expect estimated coefficients for Age to be negative and AgeSQ (age squared) to be positive.
- We expect the estimated coefficient on Endorsement contracts to be positive.
- We expect the estimated coefficient on medals earned to be positive.
- We expect the estimated coefficient on Olympic appearances to be positive.
- We expect the estimated coefficient on the gender dummy variable to be negative (Dfem = one when the swimmer is female).
  Chapter seven suggested that the best swimmers come from Cal Berkeley, Stanford, Texas, and Florida. We expect these variables to have a positive influence on swimmer earnings.

Table 10.2 reports the estimated coefficients from the basic earnings model.

Table 10.2 contains the results for the estimated coefficients that are statistically significant. The number of Olympic appearances was not significant in this sample and the swimmer's college experience did not explain much of the variation in earnings. Age has the largest economic impact on earnings. And, that impact is negative. If you are 1 year older at your peak Olympic performance, your swim earnings are 311% lower. But, note that this negative effect diminishes. If you are a female, there is more bad news: the gender gap is 249%.[4] Endorsements have the expected impact

---

[3] Note that, even when Phelps and Ledecky are included, there are no sign changes on any explanatory variables, but some results are muted. These results are available from the author upon request.

[4] Since the dependent variable is log transformed, when one of the explanatory variables changes, we can interpret the change on the left-hand-side as a change in the ratio of the expected geometric means of the original (nonlogged) swimmer earnings. The exponentiated value of −0.914 is −2.49. This means that when a swimmer is female, her earnings are 249% lower.

Table 10.2 Estimated impact on swimmer earnings

Earnings	Coeff.	Robust Std. Err.	t	P > |t|	$R_2 = 0.84$
Age	−1.133	0.349	−3.41	0.006	
AgeSQ	0.018	0.005	3.41	0.006	
Medals	0.252	0.074	3.41	0.006	
Dfem	−0.914	0.417	−2.19	0.051	
Endorse	0.328	0.110	2.97	0.013	

The dependent variable is the natural log of lifetime endorsement earnings. $N = 30$

on earnings; for each additional endorsement contract, earnings increase by 38%. Lastly, medals count. Each additional medal earned increases income by 29%. These basic results may help explain behavior observed in amateur swim athletes.

More swimmers are making the decision to give up NCAA and amateur eligibility and swim for money.[5] It makes sense that the earlier you "turn pro" the more likely you are to sign lucrative endorsement deals, the longer your pro career arc and the longer time you have to build your brand equity. Indeed, this is what Phelps did before attending the University of Michigan. However, not every top swimmer can sign enough endorsements to take this route. Some have to take the college swim path. As we discussed in chapter seven, this path is quite narrow and does not come with extra income to stash away for off-season training and Olympic dreams.

Katie Ledecky was only 19 years old in 2018. She swam for Stanford as an amateur while she competed at the Rio Olympic Games. Experts predict the value of her contract with TYR is in excess of $7 million. But, does anyone really think that is the only endorsement she will garner now that she is a professional? Barring any poor decision-making (i.e., Lochte's escapades in Rio, which lost him several lucrative contracts), Ledecky's career earnings could rival Phelps' net worth if she swims 10 to 12 more years. If she picks up even three more contracts (at $375,000 each—the average value) per year she swims, the future value of her endorsement earnings could be over $54.5 million.[6] Add to this the increased earnings from each additional Olympic medal she picks up in the next three Games, and that would put her over Phelps' net worth.

These results also reveal that male swimmers have fewer endorsement deals, on average, than their female counterparts. Yet, the females are earning less. Given the interplay between endorsements, medals and earnings, it is no surprise that a real gender gap exists in professional swim incomes. Figure 10.1 identifies the gap.

So, this gender earnings gap cannot be explained by some sort of contract discrimination. Male swimmers have two less medals than females in this sample. This should give the female swimmers the earnings edge. However, this is not what we observe. Though not conclusive, these results seem to indicate that some sort of

[5] In 2013, Michael Andrew signed with P2 Life, a sport supplement company. He was 14. He had a second contract with Mutual of Omaha that same year.

[6] Ding et al. (2011).

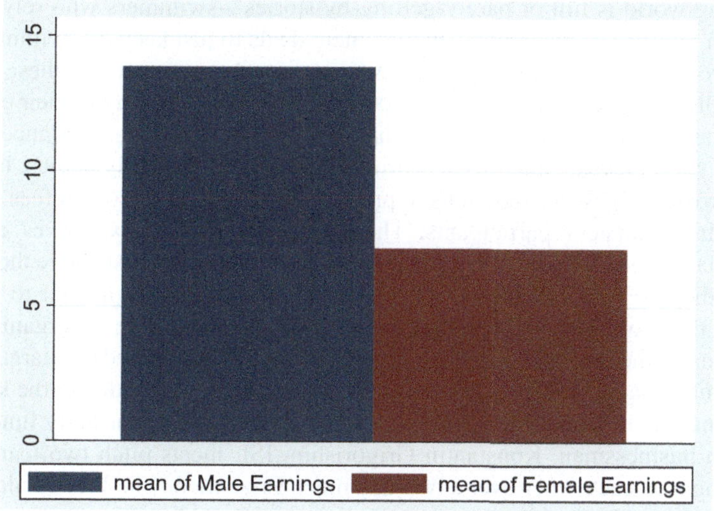

Fig. 10.1 Gender gap in elite swim. The bar chart compares the mean value of the natural log of swim earnings for males (the blue bar) and females (the red bar)

discrimination exists against the female swimmers. Clearly, more study of this important issue is warranted.

Which markets are connected to professional swim endorsement deals? Fortune reports that in 2012, 93 million people spent $1.4 billion on swimwear alone.[7] But, the endorsement contracts signed by these swimmers are not limited to swimwear alone. Nike and Under Armor retail a variety of sports apparel. Sports nutrition companies, insurance companies, jewelry, and retail food establishments also sign agreements with swimmers.

It is important to note that this study is focused on the absolute best elite performers in the sports. Many pro swimmers do not reach this level. Yet, they are still Olympians. Take the relay participants, for example. Qualified Olympic swimmers can earn a medal if they are on a preliminary heat-winning team. So, even though they don't swim in the medal-winning final race, they still are decorated with a medal because they helped the team to get to that race. What is the earning potential for this type of top swimmer?

The answer may surprise you. An Olympian earning one medal with no major endorsement deals probably earns an income below the poverty level. The best they can hope for is to finish in the top 16 swimmers (in their event) so that they can qualify for the stipend from USA Swim. Currently, this stipend is just under $3300 a month. It is virtually impossible for a top-16 ranked swimmer to hold down a job and still train at the levels required to remain competitive. Consequently, the pro

[7] http://fortune.com/2012/05/29/rich-sport-u-s-olympic-swimmers-float-on-cash accessed 06/28/2018.

swimming world is full of barely-getting-by stories—swimmers who rely on support from families or piece-meal endorsement deals to just keep on swimming.

The irony in these stories is this: USA Swim gets the money to pay these stipends from its 300,000 members who pay $100 million a year to belong to their clubs and swim. The novices literally keep the elite athletes afloat. A cursory glance at other Olympic sports reveals that this scenario is common. Organizing bodies, like USA Swim, provide necessary functions to promote the sport. They collect fees and earn income from amateur participants. The administrators and executives earn six-figure salaries, while many of the top athletes in the sport live just above the poverty level, if they are lucky. While it is true that no one forces a swim star to pursue a career in the sport, it is also true that the institutions responsible for organizing and administering the sport make the largest share of income generated by a large margin.

This may change in the future, however. This is in large part due to the launch of the International Swim League (ISL) in 2019. This league is currently funded by a Ukranian businessman, Konstantin Grigorishin. ISL meets pitch two teams of 32 athletes against each other over a two-day meet. Prize money in 2019 totaled over 4 million dollars. Half of the inaugural season meets sold out in venues that hold between 1000 to 2200 spectators. Grigorishin plans to sell expanded media rights to an American broadcast company next season.

Two legal matters related to the launch of the ISL are pending. A class action suit filed by Tom Shields and other Olympians against FINA may determine the financial fate of future swimmers. FINA initially banned swimmers from swimming in ISL (or any other nonsanctioned FINA competition). Eventually, FINA agreed it could not prevent swimmers from participating in non-FINA events. However, it is still trying to exercise control of the market by extracting fees from competitors.[8] The organizing bodies of other Olympic sports may find themselves in the same position if rival leagues form with deeper pockets for athlete pay. At the very least, feedback about the factor income shares across professional and elite sports might prove beneficial for decision-makers as they plan the future of competition.

References

Ding, H., Molchanov, A. E., & Stork, P. A. (2011). The value of celebrity endorsements: A stock market perspective. *Marketing Letters, 22*(2), 147–163.

Humphreys, B. R. (2000). Equal pay on the hardwood: The earnings gap between male and female NCAA Division I basketball coaches. *Journal of Sports Economics, 1*(3), 299–307.

Simmons, R., & Forrest, D. (2004). Buying success: Team performance and wage bills in US and European sports leagues. In R. Fort & J. Fitzel (Eds.), *International sports economics comparisons* (pp. 123–140). Santa Barbara (California): Praeger.

[8] https://www.wsj.com/articles/new-swim-league-aims-to-create-a-pro-world-outside-fo-the-olympics-11576846849 accessed 01/20/2020.

Chapter 11
What's Next for Aquatic Sports?

Jill S. Harris

Abstract Aquatic sports are not immune from challenges that plague other sports. This summary highlights a few of the key hurdles the sport must navigate in order to thrive in the decades to come. Gender and racial discrimination, sexual harassment, and abuse as well as unfair treatment by organizing bodies must be confronted.

Even as we bid farewell to Michael Phelps, Katie Ledecky is ascending to his throne. He reigned on it for over almost two decades. Ledecky is a different kind of swimmer than Phelps. She is a distance athlete, while Phelps was a short-course specialist. Ledecky competed as an amateur for Stanford while crushing at the Rio Olympics. Phelps turned pro before his college years. Still, Ledecky has the potential to crush the competition in like fashion. As the previous chapter showed, however, Ledecky is the only female swimmer capable of earning a net worth close to that of Phelps. This, perhaps, is the challenge for aquatic sport moving forward.

By the time this volume is published, familiar names will have qualified for the next international competitions and the 32nd Olympic Games in Japan. After all, at the recent Pan Am games, Michael Andrew took the 100-meter breast, while Ledecky dominated the 400-meter free. Simone Manuel broke the United States open record in the 50-meter free. Some new names are also posting record-breaking times. Kathleen Baker took the 200-meter Individual Medley with an impressive two-second gap between her and the second place finisher, and Zane Grothe did the same in the 800-meter free.

Professional swim may be positioned well to close the gender gap on multiple fronts: Equal treatment for equal performance, opportunities abounding for both genders and all races, and a culture and climate of respect and dignity. In this post-Larry Nassar world, however, USA Swim will have to clean house like other sports. Allegations of sexual misconduct and harassment have made the headlines. Over 150 male coaches are on the permanently banned list, according to a report filed by

J. S. Harris (✉)
United States Air Force Academy, Colorado Springs, CO, USA
e-mail: jill.harris@afacademy.af.edu

J. S. Harris (ed.), *The Economics of Aquatic Sports*, Sports Economics, Management and Policy 17, https://doi.org/10.1007/978-3-030-52340-4_11

National Public Radio in May of 2018.[1] In 2012, Terri McKeaver became the first female to coach at the Olympic level. Given that female competitors dove into international competition in 1912, it took 100 years to get a woman on deck. Sadly, her tenure was a short 4 years.

Still, where Phelps and Ledecky have gone, more are sure to follow. Swim superstars should beget more superstars, even if the road to that stardom is a narrow one. College swimming is not as open and competitive as it could be given NCAA rules. The NCAA is in a state of flux; social pressures and judicial pressures are coaxing change. In the not too distant future, athletes may be able to benefit from Olympic exposure and earn income from the use of their likenesses and images without sacrificing amateur status. Meanwhile, Title IX ensures that female athletes should continue to gain access to all sports, not just aquatic ones.

Swimmers want to continue to break records. The temptation to use performance-enhancing drugs (PEDs) is not going away anytime soon. Simulations from a panel data set of over 340 swimmers across 35 years illustrated that the financial gains from doping in the swimming world are probably quite small. Still, improved oversight and management of the consequences from doping may make future competitions more fair and balanced. The United States leads the way in this arena and should continue to be an exemplar for best practices in safe, ethical, and drug-free competition.

USA Water Polo women keep making big splashes internationally. Broad, open access to the sport is one key to its success. The supply of tall players in the United States seems stable (given the paucity of alternative markets for female players). This is in sharp contrast to the USA Mens' experience in the game. The steady demand for Eastern European players is likely to block would-be American males from reaching the pinnacle in the sport.

If they do, we know how to measure the productivity of players in the pool. Our wins produced model opens the door for several avenues of research. Expanding the model to include goalies will make it a more powerful resource for decision-makers in the sport as they recruit talent, develop offensive and defensive strategies, and try to win games. The economics of officiating will continue to be interesting and important to the outcome of aquatic contests. Human bias colors behavior as we learned in chapter four. Referees, coaches, players, and fans will continue to be intrigued by the idea of a "hot hand" in water polo. The latest research on this phenomenon suggests it is real and identifiable. All complex invasion sports are natural laboratories for the study of this hot topic.

How do we consume aquatic sports? For the most part, these sports are enjoyed in-person on the deck or in the stands. But, the 2018 National Swim Championships were sponsored by Phillips66. More lucrative sponsorships loom with swim's rising stars. Limited television coverage and streaming coverage is available. The market structure of aquatic sport will determine whether or not we will be able to tune in

[1] https://www.npr.org/2018/07/04/623540000/as-usa-swimming-grapples-with-sexual-abuse-athletes-cite-lack-of-female-coaches, accessed 06/25/2018.

and watch water polo or swim competitions on demand in the future. These sponsorships and expanding markets may also create more revenue opportunities for elite professional athletes as well as amateurs. For this reason, the class action suit *Shields*, et al. *v. FINA, Case No. 18-cv-07393* could be very important to the overall industry structure of international swim competition. Athletes have begun publically criticizing the distribution of income within FINA and USA Swim.[2] The success of the newly formed International Swim League will certainly be partially determined by the decision rendered in court.

Meanwhile, the next Ledecky is already enrolled in a learn-to-swim program somewhere. Michael Andrew may be the next Phelps. Ashleigh Johnson is the premier female water polo goalie in the world. Simone Manuel's star is shining bright in international sprint competitions. Aquatic sport is emerging as a more inclusive industry. To be sure, more can be done to close the earnings gap between males and females. But, today's climate and culture surrounding gender equality is almost certain to bring about incremental change.

Aquatic sports are "lifetime" sports: you will find octogenarians alongside 8 year olds in most swim lanes around the world. Perhaps, for this reason, more than any other, the economics of aquatic sports will continue to attract and invite attention from swimmers, water polo players, coaches, referees, and scholars alike.

References

As USA Swimming Grapples with Sexual Abuse, Athletes Cite Lack of Female Coaches. (2018). Access June 3, 2019. https://www.npr.org/2018/07/04/623540000/as-usa-swimming-grapples-with-sexual-abuse-athletes-cite-lack-of-female-coaches

Shields v. Fed'n Internationale de Natation, Case No. 18-cv-07393-JSC (N.D. Cal. Dec. 16, 2019).

[2] https://swimswam.com/katinka-hosszu-michael-andrew-tom-shields-file-lawsuit-against-fina/ accessed 06/03/2019.

The manufacturer's authorised representative in the EU is Springer Nature Customer Service Centre GmbH, Europaplatz 3, 69115 Heidelberg, Germany. If you have any concerns regarding our products, please contact ProductSafety@springernature.com

Printed and bound by CPI Group (UK) Ltd, Croydon, CR0 4YY
30/09/2026
02225710-0004